the italian cuisine I love

the italian cuisine I love

by JULES J. BOND

LEON AMIEL • PUBLISHER
NEW YORK

Table of Contents

Published by
LEON AMIEL • PUBLISHER
NEW YORK
ISBN 0-8148-0681-3

Printed in the United States of America

Foreword

Italy's cuisine is undoubtedly among the most varied, imaginative and oldest of Europe. Some of the great Italian dishes have their origins in Roman times, others come from the Venetians whose ships and merchants brought delicacies from faraway places back to Venice. Some were invented and prepared at the court of the Medicis. Catherine de Medici's cooks came with her to France where they taught their art to the cooks of the Court. Ice cream is an invention of Italians. The first cookbook ever printed was by an Italian and printed in Italy.

All too many people think that Italian food means only spaghetti and meat balls, eggplant parmigiana, scaloppine or pizza. Far from it. From the Alps to Sicily each region of Italy has its distinctive cuisine. The heavy use of tomatoes and cooking with oil that most people associate with Italian food is mainly found in the South. The North cooks with butter and the flavorings are less robust.

Take a cook's tour and enjoy some of Italy's splendid culinary accomplishments.

Bon appetit,

Jules Bond

LIST OF COLOR PLATES

We would like to thank Ruffino Wines (RW), the National Macaroni Institute (NMI), the Rice Council (RC), and the Italian Tourist Office (ITO) for furnishing us with color illustrations. Thanks also due to Roy Jensen who coordinated the production of this book.

Antipasti — Italian Appetizers properly served should appeal to one's eyes as well as to the taste buds. They range from the simplest to the full array of delicacies found displayed in good restaurants. Some of the simplest antipasti are among the best — such as:

Prosciutto (Italian ham) and Melon

(for 4)

¼ lb. prosciutto, sliced paper thin
1 small melon, peeled and cut into wedges

Chill melon and serve with sliced prosciutto.

Prosciutto and Figs

(for 4)

¼ lb. prosciutto
4 ripe figs

Chill figs and serve with prosciutto.

Marinated Artichoke Hearts

(for 6)

1 package frozen artichoke hearts
1½ cups dry white wine
1½ tbsp. wine vinegar
1 bay leaf
1 small clove garlic, slivered
olive oil
¼ small lemon, cut into thin slices
1 bay leaf
1 tbsp. wine vinegar
salt and pepper to taste

Combine wine, 1½ tablespoons vinegar, bay leaf and garlic and cook artichokes in this mixture until just done. Remove and drain well. Place the artichoke hearts in a jar, cover with olive oil, add sliced lemon, bay leaf, 1 tablespoon vinegar, salt and pepper, cover and marinate for at least three days.

Marinated Shrimp

(for 6 to 8)

1 stalk celery
1 carrot, peeled and sliced
1 bay leaf
3 tbsp. wine vinegar
½ tsp. oregano
1 tbsp. salt
2 cups water
1½ lbs. medium shrimp
½ cup olive oil
¼ cup lemon juice
salt and pepper to taste

Put celery, carrot, bay leaf, vinegar, oregano, salt and water in a saucepan and bring to a boil. Boil for a minute or two, then add the washed shrimp, bring to a boil again and cook the shrimp for not more than 2 minutes or until they just turn pink. Remove from fire, drain, peel and devein the shrimp as soon as they are cool enough to handle. Place them in a bowl, and pour, while they are still warm, oil and lemon juice over them. Season with salt and pepper, mix well, and marinate for at least 2 hours before serving.

Stuffed Mushrooms I

(for 4)

12 large firm mushrooms
1 tbsp. onion, minced
1 clove garlic, minced
2 tbsp. olive oil
4 anchovy filets, chopped
1 tbsp. parsley, minced
1 tsp. lemon juice
1 tbsp. tomato puree
¼ cup fresh white breadcrumbs
1 egg
salt and pepper to taste
fine dry breadcrumbs
3 tbsp. grated parmesan cheese
3 tbsp. olive oil

Remove mushroom stems carefully from caps. Wash, dry and chop the stems. Sauté onion and garlic in 1 tablespoon oil for a minute, add chopped mushroom stems and sauté for 3 or 4 minutes. Add anchovies, parsley, lemon juice and tomato puree. Stir and cook 5 minutes longer. Remove from fire, blend in breadcrumbs, the lightly beaten egg, salt and pepper. Fill the mushroom caps with the mixture, sprinkle with dry breadcrumbs and oil, top with a sprinkle of cheese. Place in an oiled baking dish and bake in 400° oven for about 15 minutes.

Stuffed Mushrooms II

(for 4)

8 large firm mushroom caps
1½ tbsp. butter
1 tbsp. minced shallots
2 sweet Italian sausages
¼ lb. ground veal
2 anchovy filets, chopped
⅓ cup soft white breadcrumbs
1 egg, lightly beaten
salt and pepper to taste
2 tbsp. parsley, chopped

Remove stems from mushroom caps, trim and chop. Brush caps with melted butter and reserve. Put the remaining butter in a skillet, add shallots, remove sausage meat from casing and sauté together with shallots for about 5 to 7 minutes until meat is browned and thoroughly cooked. Add veal and mushroom stems and sauté 3 minutes longer. Remove from heat and blend in anchovies, breadcrumbs, egg, parsley, salt and pepper. Pile this mixture in the mushroom caps and bake at 375° for about 15 minutes.

Marinated Mushrooms

1 lb. firm button mushrooms
2 cups dry white wine
olive oil
1 tbsp. grated onion
1 small clove garlic, crushed
1 tbsp. parsley, minced
1 bay leaf
1 tbsp. lemon juice
salt and pepper to taste
pinch of cayenne pepper

Put mushrooms in a bowl, cover with wine and marinate for a couple of hours. Drain well, place mushrooms in a jar, blend all other ingredients and pour into the jar to cover the mushrooms. Close jar and marinate mushrooms for 2 or 3 days before serving.

Clams Casino

(for 4)

2 dozen clams
3 tbsp. butter
3 anchovy filets (mashed)
2 tbsp. green pepper, minced
2 tbsp. canned pimento, chopped
pepper to taste
4 rashers lean bacon
coarse or rock salt

Open clams, loosen from shell, drain clams and reserve, along with one half shell for each. Cream butter and blend with mashed anchovies. Put a small pat of anchovy butter in each of 24 half clam shells, place a shucked clam on top of each, sprinkle with a little green pepper and pimento, season with pepper and cover with a small piece of bacon.

Cover the bottom of a shallow baking pan with coarse salt or rock salt, place clams on top and broil under a very hot preheated broiler, about 3 inches from the flame, for about 3 to 4 minutes.

Stuffed Tomatoes

(for 4)

4 firm, ripe tomatoes
1 cup canned tuna
¾ cup pimento-stuffed olives, chopped
2 tbsp. grated onion
1 tbsp. parsley, minced
1 tsp. capers, drained and chopped
2 anchovy filets, mashed
1 tsp. lemon juice
mayonnaise
1 tbsp. chives, chopped

Cut cap off the tomatoes, hollow out carefully. Mash tuna and combine with all other ingredients except mayonnaise and chives. Blend well. Add enough mayonnaise to bind the mixture — about ½ to ¾ cup — fill the tomato shells and sprinkle with chives. Chill before serving.

Baked Clams Posilipo

(for 4)

2 dozen clams
1 cup white breadcrumbs
1 large clove garlic, minced
1 tbsp. parsley, minced
1 tsp. oregano
½ tsp. basil
pepper to taste
1 tbsp. tomato puree
2 tbsp. grated parmesan cheese
⅓ cup olive oil

Scrub clams, open and discard one half shell of each. Mix all other ingredients except oil and put some of the mixture on each of the clams in its half shell. Sprinkle each half shell with oil and bake in 400° oven for about 10 to 12 minutes until golden brown.

Fried Anchovy Bread

(for 4)

16 slices of bread from a long loaf of French or Italian bread, cut ½ inch thick
8 thin slices of mozarella cheese
8 anchovy filets
1 cup milk
flour
2 eggs, lightly beaten with 1 tbsp. of milk
olive oil for frying (about 1 cup)
1 small jar of canned pimento

Place a slice of cheese and one anchovy filet on each of 8 slices of bread. Put a few thin strips of pimento on each. Cover with another slice of bread. Sprinkle these sandwiches on both sides with milk, then dredge in flour, dip in the egg and fry in oil until golden brown on both sides.

Egg Noodle Spinach Cheese Soup. See page 21 for recipe.→

Spring Salad with Asparagus Tips

(for each person)

1 large artichoke heart
6 asparagus tips, peeled
6 leaves Boston or other lettuce
1 thin slice of liver pâté (opt.)
2 tbsp. pine nuts
6 leaves of Belgian endive, cut in strips
½ cup finely shredded red cabbage
1 small celery heart, cut in thin strips
¼ cup shelled walnuts
1 tbsp. parsley, chopped
1 lemon
mayonnaise
oil and vinegar salad dressing

This salad is served to each person on two plates.

Cook the artichoke hearts and the asparagus in boiling salted water until just tender. Line 2 plates with lettuce leaves. Trim the artichoke heart, remove the inner leaves and the "choke" and put it in the center of one plate. Top with a slice of liver pâté. Around it arrange the asparagus tips, pine nuts and Belgian endive. On the other plate place the strips of celery heart, the red cabbage and the walnuts. Sprinkle with parsley. Scoop out the lemon, fill the shell with mayonnaise, and put it in the middle of the plate. Serve with oil and vinegar dressing on the side to be used liberally on both plates.

←*Spring Salad with Asparagus Tips.*

Cheese Croquettes

½ lb. mozarella cheese
1 tbsp. flour
1 egg
1 tbsp. parsley, minced
salt to taste
flour
1 cup olive oil

Work cheese with your hands until it begins to get soft. Add 1 tablespoon flour, egg, parsley, and salt; blend and shape the mixture in small croquettes or balls. Dredge in flour and fry in hot oil until golden brown.

You can also shape the cheese croquettes or balls around a pitted olive or a rolled anchovy filet.

Egg Noodle Spinach Cheese Soup

(for 8-10)

2 tbsp. salad oil
¾ cup chopped onion
1 large garlic clove, crushed
6 cups chicken broth
8 oz. fine egg noodles
1 tsp. salt
paprika
packaged croutons
6 cups milk
2 packages (10 oz. each) frozen chopped spinach, thawed and drained
½ lb. shredded fontina cheese (about 2 cups)
½ lb. shredded provolone cheese (about 2 cups)

In a large saucepan, heat oil. Add onion and garlic; sauté over medium heat, stirring occasionally, until onion is tender, about 5 minutes. Add chicken broth. Heat to a rapid boil. Gradually add noodles and salt. Cook uncovered, stirring occasionally, until tender, about 6 minutes. Stir in milk, spinach, and cheeses. Cook until heated through and cheese are melted, stirring constantly. Do not boil.

To serve, sprinkle each serving with paprika and croutons. Serve immediately.

Chicken and Spinach Broth

(for 4)

1 lb. fresh spinach
4 cups chicken broth
1 cup cooked chicken, diced
salt and pepper to taste
¼ tsp. grated lemon rind
3 tbsp. grated romano cheese

Trim tough stalks off spinach. Wash spinach very well and drain. Put broth in a saucepan, bring to a boil and add spinach. Cook for 6 to 7 minutes until spinach is just tender but not too soft. Add chicken, lemon rind, salt and pepper and heat through. When serving sprinkle with grated cheese.

Noodle Broccoli Cheese Soup

(for 12)

2 tbsp. oil or butter
¾ cup onion, chopped
6 cups chicken broth
8 oz. fine egg noodles (about 4 cups)
1 tsp. salt
2 packages frozen broccoli
1 clove garlic, crushed
6 cups milk
1 lb. (4 cups) American cheese, cubed
pepper to taste

In a large saucepan heat oil. Add onion and sauté over medium heat for 3 minutes. Add chicken broth, heat to boiling. Gradually add noodles and salt so that the broth continues to boil. Cook uncovered for 3 minutes, stirring occasionally. Stir in broccoli and garlic; cook 4 minutes more. Add milk, cheese and pepper and continue cooking until the cheese melts, stirring constantly.

Chick Pea Soup

(for 6)

2 tbsp. butter
¼ cup chopped onion
1 clove garlic, minced
2 tbsp. parsley, minced
½ tsp. basil
salt and pepper to taste

1 large can chick peas, drained
1 large can Italian tomatoes, chopped
4 cups chicken broth

Heat butter in a heavy saucepan, add onion, garlic and parsley, and sauté until onion is soft. Add all other ingredients, cover and simmer for 15 minutes.

Escarole Minestra

(for 4)

2 lbs. escarole
4 cups chicken broth
salt and pepper to taste
1 medium onion, sliced
1 clove garlic, chopped
4 scallions, chopped
⅓ cup lean bacon, chopped
1 large can chick peas
2 tbsp. parsley, minced
½ tsp. basil
4 tbsp. grated parmesan

Trim escarole, discard tough outer leaves and wash well. Break leaves in half, put in saucepan, add chicken broth and enough water to just cover the leaves. Season with salt and pepper, cover and cook until tender — about 15 minutes.

Drain and reserve 2 cups of the cooking liquid. Sauté bacon in a heavy saucepan, add onion, garlic and scallions and sauté until soft but not browned. Add parsley, basil, and drained chick peas; mix. Add escarole and cooking liquid and simmer for 15 minutes. Sprinkle with grated cheese when serving.

Minestrone I

(for 6)

- ¼ cup chopped salt pork
- ½ cup chopped onion
- 1 clove garlic, chopped
- 1 tbsp. parsley, minced
- ½ tsp. basil
- 3 stalks celery
- 2 medium carrots, peeled and sliced
- 2 medium potatoes, diced
- 2 cups cooked fava beans
- 2 zucchini, diced
- 1 cup green peas
- 1 green pepper, seeded and diced
- 1 cup shredded white cabbage
- 6 cups chicken broth
- 2 tbsp. tomato paste
- 1 cup pasta shells or macaroni
- salt and pepper to taste
- ⅓ cup grated parmesan cheese

Sauté salt pork in a heavy saucepan until rendered, then add onion, garlic and parsley. Stir and sauté until onion is soft. Add all other ingredients except pasta shells and cheese, cover and cook gently for about one hour. Then add pasta and cook 10 minutes until pasta is done. Sprinkle with cheese before serving.

Minestrone II

(for 6)

2 cups navy beans
1 small head white cabbage
1 cup sliced onions
2 cloves garlic, sliced
1 cup tomatoes, peeled, seeded and chopped
½ lb. lean fresh pork, cubed
2 large potatoes, quartered
6 cups chicken broth
1 tsp. basil
salt and pepper to taste

Soak beans in cold water for 3 to 4 hours. Drain and put in a heavy saucepan. Add all other ingredients, bring to a boil, cover and simmer for about 2 hours or until beans are cooked. Add more broth during cooking if needed.

Onion Soup Venetian Style

(for 4)

6 tbsp. butter
2 Bermuda onions, sliced thin
1 clove garlic, minced
2 tbsp. flour
6 cups hot chicken broth
salt and pepper to taste
3 egg yolks
½ cup grated parmesan cheese
slices of toasted French bread
2 tbsp. minced parsley

Heat butter in heavy saucepan, sauté onion and garlic until light golden brown. Add flour and cook stirring for a minute or two. Add chicken broth, salt and pepper, blend well and simmer covered for half an hour. Beat egg yolks lightly and blend in the grated cheese. Remove soup from fire, whisk in the egg yolk mixture. Put toasted bread in soup plates, ladle soup over the bread and sprinkle with parsley.

Rice and Pea Soup

(for 4)

2 tbsp. butter
1/3 cup minced onion
1/3 cup diced cooked ham
2 tbsp. parsley, minced
1 cup fresh shelled peas
(or 1 package frozen)
4 cups chicken broth
salt and pepper to taste
¾ cup long grain rice

Heat butter in heavy saucepan, add onion and sauté for a few minutes; add ham and parsley, stir and sauté for a minute; then add peas and chicken broth, season with salt and pepper and bring to a boil. Put rice in a strainer, rinse well under cold running water, add to soup, bring to a boil, cover and cook for about 15 minutes or until rice is tender.

Straciatella

Egg Soup

(for 4 to 5)

6 cups chicken broth
3 eggs
4 tbsp. grated romano cheese
2 tbsp. semolina
salt and pepper to taste
2 tbsp. minced parsley

Whisk eggs until light and frothy, blend in cheese, semolina, parsley and 2 or 3 tablespoons of cold broth.

Bring broth to a full boil, then lower flame to simmer, season with salt and pepper, add egg mixture in a thin stream, whisking continuously. When all the egg mixture has been added to the soup, remove from heat and whisk for another minute or so.

Brodetto
Fish Soup
(for 6)

3 lbs. various fish (flounder, whiting, mackerel, bass and others)
1 doz. small clams, opened, with their juice
½ lb. shrimp, shelled and deveined
1 squid, cleaned and cut into small pieces (opt.)
1 small eel, skinned and cut into pieces (opt.)
½ cup olive oil
1 cup canned peeled tomatoes, with their juice
1 tbsp. tomato paste
1½ tbsp. parsley, chopped
1 tsp. tarragon
salt and pepper to taste
½ cup dry white wine
½ cup clam juice
1 medium onion, chopped

Scale and clean fish, cut off heads and discard, cut fish into large chunks. Heat olive oil in a heavy saucepan, add onion and garlic and sauté until light golden brown. Add tomatoes, tomato paste, parsley, tarragon, white wine and clam juice; bring to a boil, add squid and eel and simmer for about 15 minutes. Add clams and shrimp, simmer 5 minutes longer, then add fish, salt and pepper and cook another 10 minutes or until fish is cooked. Put a piece of toasted Italian bread in each soup plate and ladle fish and soup over it.

Clam Soup

(for 6)

¼ cup olive oil
1 medium onion, chopped
2 cloves garlic, minced
3 anchovy filets
½ cup dry red wine
2 cups clam juice
2 cups water
4 tbsp. tomato paste
¼ tsp. oregano
pepper to taste
pinch of cayenne pepper
2 cups drained chopped clams (canned)

Heat oil in heavy saucepan, sauté onion and garlic until soft but not browned. Add wine, stir and cook until reduced by half. Add anchovies, tomato paste, clam juice, water, oregano, pepper and cayenne; blend well and simmer for 10 minutes. Add clams and heat through. Serve over toasted bread slices.

Cacciucco
Fish Soup
(for 6)

⅓ cup olive oil
¼ cup chopped onion
2 cloves garlic, minced
½ lb. shrimp, shelled, deveined and cut in pieces
⅓ cup dry white wine
1 cup clam juice
2 cups water
2 tbsp. tomato paste
1 lb. fresh cod filet, cut in chunks
½ lb. haddock or halibut, cut in pieces
1 cup whole baby clams (canned)
½ tsp. lemon rind, grated
⅛ tsp. saffron
salt and pepper to taste

Heat olive oil in a heavy casserole, add onion and garlic and sauté until light golden; add shrimp and wine, cook stirring until wine has nearly evaporated. Add clam juice, water and tomato paste, stir and simmer for 5 minutes. Add all other ingredients, blend and simmer gently for about 15 minutes or until fish is cooked and flaky. Serve over slices of toasted garlic bread.

Pizza à la Garibaldi

(for 4)

uncooked bread dough sufficient for 1 medium sized loaf
½ cup olive oil
1 cup grated parmesan cheese
2 cups stuffed green olives
1 cup black olives, pitted
12 anchovy filets, drained
2 cups tomato sauce *(p. 146)*
1 tbsp. dried marjoram

Roll out the dough into a 12-inch round, leaving the outer rim a little thicker than the center. Generously oil a baking sheet and put the dough on it. Sprinkle the dough with a little olive oil and with the grated cheese. Place the stuffed green olives, the black olives and anchovy filets neatly on the dough. Top with tomato sauce, sprinkle with marjoram and a little more olive oil. Bake in a preheated 400° oven for 25 minutes.

Pizza Garibaldi.→

Fettucine Alfredo

(for 8 to 10)

¼ cup salt
8 to 12 qts. boiling water
2 lbs. medium egg noodles
1 lb. sweet butter, softened
4 cups freshly grated parmesan cheese
1 cup heavy cream at room temperature
pepper to taste

Add ¼ cup salt to rapidly boiling water. Gradually add noodles. Cook uncovered, stirring occasionally, until tender. Drain in colander.

Place butter in hot 4-quart casserole; add noodles and toss gently. Add cheese and toss again. Pour in cream; toss. Sprinkle with freshly ground pepper.

←*Fettucine Alfredo.*

The same dough is used to make a staggering variety of pasta products, differing in sizes and in shapes; and although the same dough is used, the taste of the finished dish seems to depend often on the shape of the pasta. Spaghetti, of course, is the best known; then there is the multitude of macaroni, lasagne, conchiglie, pennone and others too numerous to mention. As varied as their shapes are the ways in which they are prepared: in the north of Italy butter and cheese are served with spaghetti more frequently than further south, where tomato sauces prevail.

Cooking pasta is very simple. Plenty of boiling salted water is the main requirement. Then add all the pasta at once, stir, cover the pot and wait until the water returns to a full boil. Then uncover the pot and cook until the pasta is *al dente,* that is, cooked through but still firm to the bite. When done, empty the contents of the pot into a colander, drain well. Put the pasta in a warmed serving dish. Add butter, cheese, or oil at this point and toss well, or cover it with the sauce that you are going to use.

Stuffed Macaroni Marinara

(for 4)

1 lb. ground lean pork
1 small onion, chopped
1 egg
¼ cup milk
½ cup soft white breadcrumbs
¼ tsp. oregano
½ tsp. basil
salt and pepper to taste
12 jumbo macaroni shells
2 cups marinara sauce *(p. 143)*
½ cup dry red wine

Sauté pork in a skillet over medium heat until lightly browned. Add onion and cook 2 minutes, stirring frequently. In a small bowl beat egg, milk, breadcrumbs, oregano, basil, salt and pepper until well blended. Stir egg mixture into pork and blend. Cook macaroni *al dente* and stuff shells with pork mixture.

Combine marinara sauce and wine, pour a small amount in a 9-inch square pan. Place shells in pan, pour remaining sauce over shells. Cover with foil and bake in 350° oven 40 minutes or until hot and bubbly.

Lasagne Sorrento Style

(for 8)

1 lb. lasagne

For the sauce:

- 4 tbsp. olive oil
- 2 cloves garlic, minced
- ½ cup onion, minced
- ¾ lb. lean pork, chopped
- ½ cup beef or chicken broth
- 2 cups tomato puree
- 4 cups canned Italian tomatoes, mashed
- 1 tbsp. sugar
- 1 tbsp. wine vinegar
- 1 tsp. crushed rosemary
- salt and pepper to taste

Heat oil in a saucepan, sauté onion and garlic until limp, add pork and sauté, stirring a few times for 15 minutes. Add all other ingredients, cover and simmer for an hour.

Bring water in a large pot to a boil, salt and add a spoonful of oil. Cook lasagne *al dente,* drain well, spread out on a towel and cool.

Prepare the *Filling:*

- 1½ lbs. ricotta cheese
- 1 lb. mozarella, sliced thin
- 3 tbsp. parsley, chopped
- 2 tbsp. fresh basil leaves, chopped (or 2 tsp. dried basil)
- 1 cup parmesan cheese, grated

Cover bottom of a square baking pan with a coating of the sauce. Cover with a layer of lasagne, top with pieces of ricotta, sprinkle with parsley and basil, top with some slices of mozarella, another layer of sauce and a sprinkle of parmesan. Continue in the same order until all ingredients are used up. Top with sauce and grated cheese. Bake in 400° oven for about 25 minutes.

Lasagne with Clam Sauce

(for 8)

4 tbsp. butter
4 tbsp. olive oil
2 cloves garlic, minced
1/3 cup onion, minced
3 cups canned minced clams (drained)
3 cups canned Italian tomatoes, mashed
½ cup clam juice (drained from minced clams)
3 anchovy filets, mashed
2 eggs, lightly beaten
2 cups ricotta cheese
2/3 cup parmesan cheese, grated
2 tbsp. parsley, chopped
1 tsp. oregano
salt and pepper to taste
1 lb. mozarella cheese, thinly sliced
1 lb. lasagne, cooked al dente, drained and cooled

Heat butter and oil in a saucepan, add garlic and onion and sauté until light golden brown. Add clams, sauté 2 minutes longer, stir in tomatoes, clam juice and anchovies, mix, cover and simmer for 15 minutes.

Blend eggs, ricotta, ½ cup of parmesan, parsley, oregano, salt and pepper. Put half of the lasagne in an oiled oblong baking dish, cover with half the clam tomato mixture, half the mixed ricotta and a layer of mozarella slices. Repeat and top with mozarella and a sprinkle of parmesan. Bake in 400° oven for about 25 minutes until browned and bubbly.

Spaghetti and Anchovy Sauce

(for 4)

1 lb. spaghetti
1 cup chopped onion
1 clove garlic, minced
1 tbsp. olive oil
8 anchovy filets, crushed
2 cups canned Italian tomatoes (drained), chopped
¼ lb. fresh mushrooms, chopped
¼ cup pitted green olives, sliced
2 tbsp. parsley, chopped
½ tsp. oregano
½ tsp. rosemary
½ cup dry white wine
salt and pepper to taste
¼ cup grated parmesan cheese

Heat oil in a saucepan, sauté onion and garlic until light golden brown, add anchovies, sauté 2 minutes longer, add tomatoes, mushrooms, olives, herbs, salt and pepper, blend well and simmer for 15 minutes. Add wine and simmer 5 minutes longer.

Cook spaghetti al dente, drain, pour sauce over spaghetti, sprinkle with cheese and serve.

Spaghetti Carbonara

(for 4)

1 lb. spaghetti
2 tbsp. salt
4-6 qts. boiling water
½ cup butter
½ lb. bacon, chopped
2 cups smoked or cooked ham, diced
1 large onion, chopped
2 cloves garlic, chopped
½ lb. mushrooms, sliced
½ cup dry white wine
1 cup (½ pint) heavy cream
2 eggs, well beaten
¼ cup chopped parsley
salt to taste
freshly grated parmesan or romano cheese

Gradually add spaghetti and 2 tablespoons salt to rapidly boiling water. Cook uncovered, until tender. Drain.

While spaghetti is cooking, melt butter in a large skillet and sauté bacon and ham until golden brown. Add onion and garlic and continue to sauté for 5 minutes. Add mushrooms and sauté for 1 minute. Stir in wine. Beat cream and eggs together until well blended. Stir mixture into skillet. Drain spaghetti and add to sauce with parsley. Stir over low heat. Season to taste with salt. Serve piping hot sprinkled with desired cheese.

Spaghetti in Garlic Sauce

(for 4)

1 lb. spaghetti
8 tbsp. butter
8 tbsp. olive oil
3 large cloves garlic, finely minced
4 tbsp. parsley, minced
½ tsp. basil
½ tsp. marjoram
pinch of dried red pepper
salt and pepper to taste
grated parmesan cheese

Heat butter and oil in a saucepan. Sauté garlic until it just starts to color but do not brown. Add parsley, basil, marjoram, red pepper, salt and pepper, and heat through.

Cook spaghetti al dente, drain, put in hot serving dish, add sauce and toss. Top with grated cheese and serve cheese also on the side.

Spaghetti with Ham and Eggs

(for 4)

1 lb. spaghetti
3 tbsp. butter
½ lb. cooked ham, chopped
2 tbsp. onion, minced
2 eggs, lightly beaten
1 tbsp. parsley, minced
2 scallions, minced
salt and pepper to taste
½ cup grated romano cheese

While spaghetti is cooking, sauté onions and ham in butter for a few minutes until lightly browned. When spaghetti is cooked, drain and blend in immediately the eggs, ham, parsley, scallions, season with salt and pepper, toss, add cheese and toss again before serving.

Note: The heat of the spaghetti actually cooks the eggs.

Spaghetti and Meat Balls

(for 4)

½ lb. lean pork, ground
½ lb. veal, ground
¼ lb. cooked ham, ground
1 large clove garlic, minced
2 tbsp. onion, grated
2 tbsp. parsley, chopped
salt and pepper to taste
⅔ cup white breadcrumbs
1 large egg, lightly beaten
¼ cup milk
¼ cup flour

¼ cup olive oil
1 medium onion, chopped
4 cups canned Italian tomatoes
½ tsp. oregano
½ tsp. basil
½ tsp. rosemary
salt and pepper to taste
½ cup dry white wine
2 tbsp. tomato paste
1 lb. spaghetti

Blend pork, veal, ham, garlic, grated onion, parsley, salt, pepper, egg, breadcrumbs, and milk; shape into 8 balls. Heat oil in a saucepan, dredge meat balls in flour and fry until well browned on all sides. Remove meat balls from pan and keep warm. Sauté chopped onion in the same pan until light golden brown; add tomatoes, herbs, season with salt and pepper and simmer for half an hour. Then add wine, tomato paste, blend well, return meat balls to sauce and simmer gently for half an hour longer.

Cook spaghetti al dente, drain, put in a serving dish, pour sauce over spaghetti and top with meat balls.

Spaghetti and Sausages

(for 4)

1 lb. spaghetti
¾ lb. sweet Italian sausages
¼ lb. hot Italian sausages
1 cup onions, chopped
2 cloves garlic, minced
¾ lb. mushrooms, thickly sliced
2 tbsp. parsley, chopped
3 cups canned Italian tomatoes, crushed
½ cup dry white wine
salt and pepper to taste
¼ cup grated romano cheese

Remove sausage meat from casing and sauté in a saucepan for a few minutes, add onions and garlic and continue cooking until onions are light golden brown. Add mushrooms and sauté 5 minutes longer. Add parsley, tomatoes, salt, pepper, and wine, blend and cook gently until sauce has thickened.

Cook spaghetti al dente, drain and place in a buttered or oiled casserole, pour the sauce over the spaghetti, blend lightly with a fork, sprinkle with grated cheese and bake in 325° oven for about 30 minutes until top is well browned.

Spaghetti with White Clam Sauce

(for 4)

4 doz. medium clams or 2 cups canned minced clams and 3 cups clam juice
1 cup chopped onion
4 to 5 cloves garlic, minced
½ cup chopped parsley
½ cup butter
1 tsp. salt
1 tsp. dried basil leaves
freshly ground pepper to taste
1 lb. spaghetti
2 tbsp. salt

Wash clams thoroughly. In large pot, cook clams covered in small amount of water just until they open. Remove clams. Strain the broth and reserve 3 cups. Remove clams from shells; chop. In large skillet or Dutch oven sauté onion, garlic and parsley in melted butter until onion is almost tender; add clams and reserved broth, 1 teaspoon salt, basil and pepper. Boil 1 minute.

Meanwhile, gradually add spaghetti and 2 tablespoons salt to rapidly boiling water so that water continues to boil. Cook uncovered, stirring occasionally, until tender. Drain in colander. Serve in shallow bowels topped with clam sauce.

Spaghetti with Chicken Liver Sauce

(for 6)

4 tbsp. butter
1 cup chopped onion
2 cloves garlic, crushed
1/3 cup chopped parsley
salt and pepper to taste
1½ tsp. oregano
¼ tsp. crushed thyme
1 tsp. worcestershire
1 can (17 oz.) plum tomatoes
1 can (6 oz.) tomato paste
1½ cups beef broth
1 lb. chicken livers, sliced
1 lb. spaghetti
½ cup grated parmesan cheese

Melt 2 tablespoons of the butter in large skillet over medium heat; add onion and garlic and sauté until tender. Reserve 1 tablespoon of the parsley for garnish; add remaining parsley, 1 teaspoon salt, other seasonings, tomatoes, tomato paste and broth to onion mixture. Cover and cook over low heat 30 minutes, stirring occasionally.

Sauté the livers in remaining 2 tablespoons butter for 5 minutes over low heat; add to sauce. Simmer sauce, uncovered, about 5 minutes more, stirring occasionally.

Meanwhile, cook spaghetti until tender. Drain in colander. Blend half of the cheese into chicken liver sauce. Serve with spaghetti sprinkled with reserved cheese and parsley.

Spaghetti in Tuna Sauce

(for 4)

1 large clove garlic, minced
2 tbsp. grated onion
5 tbsp. olive oil
2 tbsp. parsley, minced
½ tsp. basil
1½ cups Italian tomatoes, mashed, measured with their juice
1 tbsp. lemon juice
3 anchovy filets, mashed
1¼ can tuna packed in oil, drained
1 tbsp. small capers, drained
salt and pepper to taste
2 tbsp. butter
1 lb. spaghetti, cooked al dente

Heat olive oil in a saucepan, add garlic and onion and sauté until light golden. Stir in parsley and basil, add tomatoes and their juice, blend and simmer for half an hour. Crush tuna with a fork, blend into tomato sauce along with lemon juice, anchovies, capers, salt and pepper, heat through. Remove sauce from fire, swirl in the butter and pour the sauce over the hot spaghetti.

Spaghetti with Mussels

(for 4)

3 doz. mussels, scrubbed
4 shallots, minced
1 small onion, minced
1 clove garlic, mashed
1 tsp. parsley, minced
1 cup dry white wine
3 peppercorns, crushed
2 tbsp. butter
2 tbsp. flour
½ cup heavy cream
2 egg yolks
1 lb. spaghetti
1 cup grated parmesan cheese

Put the shallots, onion, garlic, and parsley into a kettle with the wine and the crushed peppercorns. Add the mussels, cover tightly and cook over high heat until the mussel shells are open, about 5 minutes. Remove from heat and cool to lukewarm. Drain the mussels and reserve all the liquid. Shell the mussels, being careful to save all the liquid that drains from the shells, and keep them barely warm. Boil the mussel liquid over moderate heat for 5 minutes and strain it twice through a very fine sieve or a triple layer of damp cheese cloth.

Heat the butter in a saucepan, stir in the flour and cook until golden. Stir in the strained liquid and simmer for 10 minutes. Beat together the heavy cream and the egg yolks and stir into the sauce off the heat. Return it to low heat, but do not let it boil or it will curdle.

Cook the spaghetti al dente. Drain carefully and toss quickly with the sauce. Add the reserved mussels and serve immediately with the grated cheese on the side.

Spaghetti with Veal and Peppers

(for 8)

2 lbs. boneless veal shoulder, cut in strips
flour
¼ cup butter
⅓ cup olive oil
4 medium green peppers, cut in strips
2 small onions, sliced
4 cloves garlic, minced
2 cans (19 oz. each) tomatoes
2 cans (8 oz. each) tomato sauce
salt and pepper to taste
1½ tsp. basil
¼ to ½ tsp. oregano
1 lb. spaghetti

Coat veal with flour; brown in butter and oil in large skillet. Remove meat; sauté green peppers and onion about 5 minutes. Return meat; add garlic, tomatoes, sauce, salt, herbs and pepper. Simmer covered 1 hour, stirring occasionally, until meat is tender.

Cook spaghetti until tender. Drain in colander. Serve with veal and pepper sauce.

Spaghetti with Veal and Peppers.→

Frittata with Cheese

(Italian Omelet)

(for 4)

Note: Frittatas have nothing in common with French omelets but the eggs. A frittata is never folded, is perfectly flat and round, prepared over low heat and must be cooked on both sides. Unless one attempts to flip the frittata over with a toss of the skillet, it is best to turn it over on a plate and slide it back in the pan, or to put the pan for a few seconds under a medium broiler without turning the eggs. A frittata should not be browned, just golden in color.

6 large eggs
salt and pepper to taste
1 tsp. paprika
¾ cup grated parmesan cheese
4 tbsp. butter

Beat eggs until well blended, add salt, pepper, paprika and cheese and beat to blend. Heat butter in a skillet until it starts to foam but do not let brown. Add the eggs and turn heat down to simmer. Cook for about 15 minutes until the eggs have set but the surface is still slightly runny. Then either flip the frittata or put for about 15 seconds under a broiler until surface is just set.

←*Spaghetti with Chicken Liver Sauce. See page 49 for recipe.*

Frittata with Peppers and Sausage

(for 4)

2 tbsp. butter
½ cup sliced onion
3 tbsp. green peppers, chopped
2 tbsp. pimento, chopped
1 large ripe tomato, peeled, seeded and chopped
1 tbsp. green olives, chopped
2 anchovy filets, mashed
1 tsp. basil
salt and pepper to taste
6 large eggs
3 tbsp. parmesan cheese, grated
3 tbsp. butter
6 sweet Italian sausages, fried and fully cooked

Heat 2 tablespoons butter in a skillet, add onion and sauté until onion is soft and light golden. Add pepper, pimento, tomato, olives, anchovy filets, basil, salt and pepper; blend well and simmer for 10 to 15 minutes, stirring a few times. Remove from fire, remove vegetables with a slotted spoon and put in a bowl to cool. Beat eggs until well blended, add parmesan, beat again and then blend in the vegetable mixture. Heat 3 tablespoons butter in a skillet and proceed to cook as in frittata with cheese *(p. 55).* Serve garnished with sausages.

Meat and Potato Frittata

(for 4 to 6)

2 cups cooked meat, diced
4 large potatoes, cooked and diced
1 large onion, sliced thin
1 clove garlic, minced
salt and pepper to taste
½ tsp. basil
2 tbsp. butter
6 large eggs, beaten
3 tbsp. butter

Heat butter in a skillet, add onions and garlic and sauté until golden brown. Add meat, potatoes, season with salt, pepper and basil, mix gently and sauté until meat and potatoes are nicely browned. Remove from heat and cool. When cool, blend with eggs and proceed to cook as in frittata with cheese *(p. 55)*.

Deep Fried Stuffed Eggs

(for 4)

4 hard-boiled eggs
1 cup ricotta cheese
2 tbsp. Romano cheese, grated
2 mashed anchovy filets
1 tsp. grated onion
salt and pepper to taste
flour
2 eggs lightly beaten
fine dry breadcrumbs
oil for deep frying

Cut eggs lengthwise in half, remove yolk. Mash and blend yolk with ricotta and Romano cheese, anchovy, onion, salt and pepper. Fill the egg halves with this mixture and mound each half with the stuffing to look like a whole egg. Roll each half in flour, dip in beaten egg and coat with breadcrumbs. Fry in deep oil until golden brown.

Clams Marinara

(for 4)

4 doz. clams
1/3 cup water
1/3 cup dry white wine
1 small bay leaf
¼ tsp. thyme
½ tsp. oregano
1 tbsp. parsley, coarsely chopped
1 tbsp. onion, chopped
2 cups marinara sauce *(p. 143)*

Put all ingredients except clams in a large saucepan or clam steamer and bring to a boil. Simmer for 5 minutes. Wash clams in cold water, scrub well to remove any sand. Add clams, cover and steam for about 10 minutes until the shells are open. Remove from heat, remove clams from shells and keep warm. Strain clam juice into a saucepan, and reduce over high heat by about half the volume. Add a cup of the reduced broth to the marinara sauce, along with the shucked clams, heat through and serve with spaghetti or rice.

Filet of Flounder Florentine

(for 4)

½ cup dry white wine
½ cup dry vermouth
½ cup clam juice
4 large flounder (or sole) filets
3 tbsp. butter
2 tbsp. flour
salt and pepper to taste
1½ tsp. tarragon
2 cups cooked spinach, drained and chopped
¼ cup parmesan cheese, grated

Combine wine, vermouth and clam juice in a large shallow saucepan or skillet, bring to a boil, add the fish filets and poach them for 2 or 3 minutes. Remove them carefully with a spatula and keep warm. Reduce the poaching liquid by about half. In another pan melt 2 tablespoons butter, add the flour and cook, stirring, for 2 or 3 minutes. Do not let brown. Add the reduced sauce, salt and pepper and tarragon, blend well and simmer while stirring until the sauce has thickened, about 3 or 4 minutes. Arrange filets in a well buttered baking dish, coat with the sauce, sprinkle with the grated cheese, surround with cooked spinach, and bake in a preheated 425° oven for about 3 to 4 minutes until top is browned and the fish flaky.

Fritto Misto
(Fried Seafood Platter)
(for 6)

1 cup flour
½ tsp. salt
⅛ tsp. white pepper, ground
3 tbsp. oil
¾ cup water
1 egg white, beaten stiff
12 shucked oysters, drained
½ lb. squid, cleaned and cut into rings (opt.)
1½ lbs. mixed fish filets (sole, weakfish, halibut, bass or others) cut in pieces
½ lb. shrimp, shelled and deveined
1 small eel, skinned and cut into pieces (opt.)
oil for deep frying

Blend flour, salt, pepper and oil, mix well. Add the water gradually, blend again and let the batter rest for an hour or two. Before using, fold beaten egg white into the batter. Coat seafood with batter and fry in oil until golden brown. Drain on paper towel. Garnish with parsley sprigs and lemon wedges before serving.

Baked Halibut

(for 4)

2 lbs. halibut
¾ cup chopped onion
1 clove garlic, chopped
2 tbsp. olive oil
¼ cup dry white wine
¼ cup water
salt and pepper to taste
1½ cups canned tomatoes, chopped
¼ tsp. thyme
½ tsp. oregano
1½ tbsp. flour
3 tbsp. coarsely chopped pitted green olives
3 tbsp. coarsely chopped pitted ripe olives
2 tbsp. capers, drained
2 tbsp. parsley, chopped
⅓ cup celery, white part only, minced

Heat oil in a saucepan, add onion and garlic and sauté until golden brown. Add wine, water, salt, pepper, tomatoes, thyme and oregano, cover and simmer for half an hour. Dilute flour with a little water, stir into the simmering sauce and cook for another 2 or 3 minutes, then add the olives, celery, capers and parsley. Blend well. Put halibut in a greased baking dish, pour the sauce over it and bake in a preheated 375° oven for half an hour. Baste a few times.

Broiled Mackerel

(for 4)

2 medium mackerel
4 tbsp. olive oil
1 large clove garlic, crushed
1 tbsp. parsley, minced
½ tsp. basil
½ tsp. oregano
¼ tsp. rosemary, crushed
2 tbsp. grated onion
pinch of cayenne pepper (opt.)
1 tsp. dijon mustard
2 tbsp. lemon juice
salt and pepper to taste

Have mackerel cleaned, split and boned. Blend all other ingredients. Put mackerel on an oiled broiler rack, skin side down. Brush fish with oil and herb mixture, broil for about 10 minutes until done and browned. Brush with mixture once or twice while broiling. Coat with remaining mixture before serving.

Lobster Fra Diavolo

(for 3)

3 lobsters, 1¼ lbs. each
⅓ cup olive oil
2 cloves garlic, minced
3 tbsp. onion, minced
½ cup dry white wine
2 cups canned Italian tomatoes
1 tbsp. vinegar
1 tbsp. chopped fresh basil (or 1 tsp. dry)
¼ tsp. thyme
1 tsp. marjoram
½ tsp. crushed red pepper (or to taste)
salt and pepper to taste
½ cup clam juice

Have lobsters split, the tails cut into two or three pieces and the carcass in half again, and the claws cracked. Remove the sack near the eyes and reserve liver and coral, if any.

Heat olive oil in a saucepan, add lobster pieces, season with salt and pepper and sauté, stirring frequently until all pieces are bright red. Sprinkle with onion and garlic, add wine, stir and cook until most of the wine has evaporated. Add all other ingredients, stir well, cover and simmer for about 15 minutes. Add more clam juice if lobster looks too dry.

Broiled Shrimp

(for 6)

1½ lbs. medium shrimp, shelled and deveined
3 tbsp. olive oil
3 tbsp. corn oil
½ cup dry white bread-crumbs (sieve before using to have them as fine as possible
1 small clove garlic, minced
1 tbsp. onion, grated
1 tbsp. lemon juice
1 tbsp. parsley, minced
salt and pepper to taste

Combine in a bowl oils and breadcrumbs, blend well. The mixture should have the consistency of heavy cream. Add shrimp to bowl; mix to coat them well, then add all other ingredients and mix again. Let stand for half an hour. Preheat the broiler for 15 minutes. Thread shrimp on skewers and broil, turning them once, for about 2 minutes for each side.

Shrimp Riviera

(for 4)

4 tbsp. butter
½ cup thinly sliced onion
1 sweet red pepper, seeded and chopped
1 firm, ripe tomato, skinned and quartered
½ cup dry vermouth
¼ cup pimento-stuffed olives, cut in half
20 jumbo shrimp, shelled and deveined
salt and pepper to taste
pinch of cayenne pepper

Melt butter in a saucepan, add onion and pepper and sauté for a few minutes until vegetables are soft but not browned. Add tomato, olives and vermouth, cover and simmer gently for 5 minutes. Add shrimp, season with salt, pepper and cayenne and cook uncovered over medium flame while stirring for about 6 to 7 minutes, or until shrimp turns pink. Do not overcook. Serve over toast or with rice.

Shrimp "Scampi"

*(for 4)**

2½ lbs. jumbo shrimp, shelled and deveined
4 tbsp. butter
4 tbsp. olive oil
salt and pepper to taste
3 cloves garlic, minced
4 tbsp. parsley, chopped

Heat oil and butter in a skillet, add shrimp and sauté over a brisk fire for about 5 minutes, while shaking the pan. Sprinkle with salt and pepper. Remove the shrimp and keep hot. Add garlic and parsley to the remaining oil in the pan, stir and sauté for half a minute and pour over shrimp. Serve with lemon wedges.

**Note*

We have included this dish under the name "scampi" with some misgivings. It seems the name scampi means, in the minds of most people, a way of cooking shrimp. Scampi, however, are crustaceans, no more related to shrimp than a lobster is. Called scampi in Italy, langoustines in France, Dublin prawn in England, they have a flavor all of their own, and anyone who has been lucky enough to taste them in Venice or Trieste, where they are at their best, will be well aware that no shrimp can come close to the splendid taste of scampi.

Shrimp Marinara

(for 4)

2 lbs. medium shrimp, shelled and deveined
2 stalks celery, cut in pieces
1 small onion, sliced
1 bay leaf
1 clove garlic, sliced
1 tsp. salt
10 peppercorns
1 cup dry white wine
3 cups water
2 cups marinara sauce *(p. 143)*

Combine celery, onion, bay leaf, garlic, salt, peppercorns, wine and water, cover and simmer for 15 minutes. Strain into another pan and discard vegetables. Bring liquid to a boil again, add shrimp and simmer for 10 minutes. In the meantime, heat the Marinara sauce; when shrimp are done, drain them, combine with the sauce, heat through and serve.

Stuffed Squid

(for 4)

8 small squid
½ cup chopped fresh mushrooms
1 tbsp. parsley, chopped
⅓ cup fresh breadcrumbs
½ tsp. oregano
2 tbsp. parmesan cheese, grated
1 egg, lightly beaten
¼ cup olive oil
1 clove garlic, minced
½ cup tomatoes, peeled, seeded and chopped
½ cup dry white wine
salt and pepper to taste

Have squid cleaned. Wash well, inside and out. Rub off the skin, cut tentacles off, discard heads and chop tentacles very fine.

Combine mushrooms, parsley, breadcrumbs, oregano, cheese, egg, chopped tentacles, and about half of the oil. Fill the squid with this mixture. Do not stuff too tight since squid shrinks considerably during cooking. Close opening with toothpicks or sew closed. Heat remaining oil in a saucepan and brown the squid lightly on all sides. Then arrange them in a single layer in the pan, add garlic, tomatoes, wine, salt and pepper, cover and simmer for about half an hour.

Rolled Breast of Chicken

(for 4)

2 tbsp. onion, minced
2 cloves garlic, minced
2 tbsp. oil
4 sweet Italian sausages
¼ cup fresh white breadcrumbs
1 tbsp. parsley, chopped
1 tsp. tarragon
salt and pepper to taste
2 large whole chicken breasts
2 tbsp. butter
½ cup dry white wine

Have chicken breasts skinned, boned and halved, and then cut horizontally in half. You will then have 8 pieces of thin chicken, the shape and size of half a chicken breast.

Heat oil in a skillet, add onion and garlic and sauté for 1 minute. Strip sausage meat out of the casing, add to skillet and cook for about 8 minutes until well browned and cooked. Break up any lumps with a fork. Remove sausage, onions and garlic with a slotted spoon, and discard all but 1 tablespoon of fat from the skillet. Mix sausage, onion, garlic with breadcrumbs, parsley, tarragon, salt and pepper and put a pat of this stuffing on each of the chicken pieces. Roll them up, tuck in the ends and secure with toothpicks or tie with thread. Add butter to skillet, sauté the chicken rolls until browned on all sides. This should take no more than 2 or 3 minutes — enough time to cook the thin pieces of chicken. Remove rolls from skillet to a hot serving platter and remove thread or toothpicks. Add wine to skillet, deglaze quickly and pour sauce over chicken rolls.

Rolled Breast of Chicken.→

Stuffed Macaroni Marinara. See page 39 for recipe.→

IMPORTED
CHIANTI

1973
CHIANTI
RUFFINO
CHIANTI RUFFINO

Breast of Chicken Piccata

(for 4)

4 tbsp. butter
1 tbsp. cooking oil
2 whole chicken breasts
flour
salt and pepper to taste
3 tbsp. freshly squeezed lemon juice
1 tbsp. butter
3 tbsp. parsley
thin slices of lemon

Have chicken breasts boned, and halved, flatten the halves between sheets of wax paper, and sprinkle the breasts lightly with flour. Heat butter and oil in a skillet. When foaming, sauté chicken breasts for 2 to 3 minutes on each side until nicely browned. Remove and keep warm. Add lemon juice, salt and pepper to skillet, deglaze to dissolve all brown particles. If needed, add a spoonful of water or dry white wine. Add one tablespoon butter, parsley, blend, return chicken breasts to pan and heat through for one minute. Put meat on a hot serving platter. Pour pan juices over the breasts and top each with a slice of lemon.

←*Spaghetti with White Clam Sauce. See page 48 for recipe.*

←*Noodle Broccoli Cheese Soup. See page 23 for recipe.*

Chicken Breasts Parmigiana

(for 4)

2 chicken breasts, skinned, boned, and cut in half
flour
salt and pepper to taste
2 eggs lightly beaten with 1 tbsp. milk
¾ cup fine white dry breadcrumbs (unseasoned)
⅓ cup grated parmesan cheese
⅓ cup butter
2 tbsp. oil

Combine breadcrumbs with grated parmesan. Flatten the chicken breast halves slightly between sheets of wax paper. Season flour with salt and pepper. Dredge breasts lightly in flour — shake off any excess. Dip them in the beaten eggs and then in the breadcrumb mixture. Be sure that they are well coated. Let them stand for half an hour before cooking. Heat butter and oil in a skillet, sauté breats quickly until nicely browned on both sides — about 3 minutes per side. Serve with lemon wedges.

Chicken Cacciatore

(for 4)

one 4-lb. frying chicken,
 cut in pieces
flour
4 tbsp. oil
2 thick slices of meaty
 bacon, diced
½ cup onion, chopped
1 clove garlic, minced
½ cup sliced mushrooms
1 tbsp. chopped parsley
¼ cup carrot, chopped fine
1 bay leaf
1 tsp. basil
2 cups canned tomatoes,
 measured, drained
½ cup dry white wine
salt and pepper to taste

Dredge chicken in flour. Heat oil in saucepan and sauté chicken pieces until browned. Remove and keep warm. Add bacon, onion and garlic to saucepan, sauté until onions are soft and transparent, add mushrooms and cook one minute more. Add parsley, carrot, bay leaf, basil and tomatoes; season with salt and pepper, blend and bring to a boil. Add chicken pieces and wine, cover and simmer for half an hour or until chicken is tender.

Chicken Lucca Style

(for 4)

one 4-lb. frying chicken, cut in serving pieces
2 tbsp. olive oil
1 tbsp. butter
3 cloves garlic, sliced
3 tbsp. chopped onion
salt and pepper to taste
1 tbsp. tomato paste
2 tbsp. canned pimento, chopped
¼ cup water
¾ cup dry white wine
1 tbsp. wine vinegar
1½ tbsp. parsley, chopped
16 pimento-stuffed green olives, sliced
16 black olives, pitted and chopped
3 anchovy filets, mashed

Heat oil and butter in a shallow saucepan. Add onion and garlic, sauté for a minute, then add chicken pieces and sauté until nicely browned on all sides. Add tomato paste, water, wine and vinegar, blend well and let come to a boil. Add olives, parsley, pimento and anchovies; mix well, season with salt and pepper, cover and cook gently for about 45 minutes until chicken is done. Uncover, and if the sauce is too thin reduce quickly.

Chicken Piemontese

(for 4)

2 tbsp. dried Italian mushrooms
½ cup hot water
one 4-lb. frying chicken, cut in serving pieces
2 tbsp. butter
1 tbsp. olive oil
2 tbsp. brandy
¾ cup chopped onion
1 large clove garlic, minced
1 small green pepper, seeded and diced
½ cup diced celery stalk
½ tsp. basil
½ tsp. rosemary
salt and pepper to taste
½ cup tomato puree

Wash mushrooms, put in a bowl and soak in half cup of hot water for an hour before starting to cook. Heat butter and oil in a saucepan, sauté chicken pieces until nicely browned, then pour brandy into the pan and flame. Remove chicken and keep warm. Put onion and garlic in the pan, sauté for two minutes, then add mushrooms and the water they soaked in, along with all other ingredients. Stir well, bring to a boil, return chicken to pan. Cover and simmer for about 45 minutes until chicken is done. If sauce is too thin reduce quickly before serving.

Chicken alla Romana

(for 4)

one 3-lb. frying chicken, cut in serving pieces
¼ cup flour
2 tbsp. butter
3 tbsp. olive oil
2 thick slices cooked ham, about ½ lb., diced
2 cloves garlic, chopped
¾ cup dry white wine
1 cup canned tomatoes, chopped
1 tsp. sugar
1 medium onion, sliced very thin
1 large sweet red pepper, cut in rings, (or green, if red pepper not available)
½ lb. firm mushrooms, sliced
1 medium zucchini, sliced
1 tbsp. very small capers, drained
½ tsp. basil
½ tsp. tarragon
salt and pepper to taste

Heat oil and butter in a saucepan, sprinkle chicken pieces with flour and sauté until well browned. Remove from pan and keep warm. Add ham to saucepan, cook while stirring for a few minutes, remove and keep warm. Add garlic to pan, sauté a minute, add wine and stir well to dissolve the brown particles in the pan and reduce the wine by half. Then add all other ingredients, mix and bring to a boil. Return chicken and ham to pan, cover and cook gently for about half an hour or until chicken is done.

Broiled Chicken

(for 2)

2½ lb. broiling chicken, split in half
¼ cup olive oil
¼ cup melted butter
1 large clove garlic, minced
¼ cup fresh lemon juice
½ tsp. grated lemon rind
½ tsp. rosemary, crushed
½ tsp. marjoram
½ bay leaf
1 tbsp. parsley, chopped
salt and pepper to taste
1 tsp. sugar

Remove breastbone of chicken and flatten the halves with a cleaver. Combine all other ingredients, blend well and rub into the chicken. Let stand for half an hour before cooking. Heat broiler, put chicken 6 inches below the flame and broil, about 8 to 10 minutes on each side. Brush with marinade during broiling.

If broiling over charcoal, don't have chicken too close to coal to avoid burning.

Chicken Livers Marsala

(for 4)

1 lb. chicken livers
salt and pepper
1 tsp. fresh sage
  (½ tsp. dried)
4 tbsp. butter
2 slices lean bacon, diced
¼ cup dry marsala wine
toast triangles

Trim livers and cut them in half. Season with sage, salt and pepper. Heat butter in skillet, add diced bacon, sauté for one minute, then add chicken livers and cook over medium flame for 3 or 4 minutes, turning them once or twice. When browned, remove to a hot serving platter, add marsala to skillet, stir to deglaze pan and simmer sauce for 2 minutes. Arrange livers on toast triangles, pour the sauce over them and serve.

Braised Stuffed Turkey

(for 8)

10 lb. turkey
1 lb. veal, ground
½ lb. sweet Italian sausage
⅓ cup bacon, diced
2 eggs, lightly beaten
1 cup bread croutons
½ cup grated Romano cheese
1 cup boiled chestnuts, peeled and mashed
turkey giblets, boiled and chopped
¼ cup dry vermouth
salt and pepper to taste
pinch of grated nutmeg
4 tbsp. butter
3 slices prosciutto ham
½ tsp. rosemary
1 pinch thyme
1 tsp. juniper berries
¾ cup dry white wine
1 tbsp. flour
1 cup chicken broth

Strip the sausage meat out of the casing, break it up and blend with veal, bacon, eggs, croutons, cheese, chestnuts, giblets, vermouth, salt, pepper and nutmeg. Stuff the turkey with this mixture and close the opening. Heat butter in a large heavy pot or Dutch oven, put the turkey in the pot and brown on all sides. Then put prosciutto over the turkey breast, add rosemary, thyme, juniper berries and wine, cover and cook over gentle heat for about 4 hours or until done. Baste quite frequently. When done, remove turkey to hot serving dish. Blend flour into sauce and add enough chicken broth to make a gravy. Simmer until thickened.

Veal Birds

(for 6)

8 thin veal cutlets
8 slices prosciutto
$^{2}/_{3}$ cup grated parmesan cheese
8 anchovy filets
flour
3 tbsp. butter
1 tbsp. olive oil
¼ cup dry white wine
8 pimento-stuffed olives
1 tbsp. parsley, chopped
1 tbsp. lemon juice
salt and pepper to taste

Trim cutlets evenly, place a slice of prosciutto on top of each, sprinkle with parmesan cheese and place one filet of anchovy on each. Roll and fasten securely with toothpicks or with thread. Season with salt and pepper and dredge rolls lightly in flour. Shake off excess flour.

Heat butter and oil in a skillet, sauté rolls until nicely browned on all sides. Add wine and lemon juice, cover and cook over medium heat about 15 to 20 minutes until rolls are cooked. Baste and turn frequently. Five minutes before they are done, add olives and parsley. Put on a serving platter, remove toothpicks or thread, add a little more wine to sauce if needed and pour over veal birds.

Braised Veal Chops

(for 4)

4 loin veal chops (2 inches thick)
flour
3 tbsp. butter
1 tbsp. oil
salt and pepper to taste
1 cup dry white wine
1½ cups chicken broth
1 medium carrot, chopped
1 medium onion, chopped
1 stalk celery, chopped
1 small clove garlic, minced
1 anchovy filet, mashed
1 tbsp. parsley, chopped
½ tsp. tarragon
½ tsp. rosemary

Dredge chops lightly in flour. Season with salt and pepper. Heat butter and oil in a saucepan, brown chops on both sides over gentle heat. Add wine and cook until wine has nearly evaporated. Turn the chops a few times while cooking. Add chicken broth, half a cup at a time, stir and continue cooking for about 15 minutes. Remove chops from pan, add all other ingredients, place chops on top, cover and cook for another half hour. Remove chops and put on a hot serving dish. Strain sauce through a sieve, if too thin reduce quickly over high flame. Correct seasoning and pour sauce over chops.

Veal Piccata

(for 4)

1½ lbs. veal scaloppine, pounded thin (about 12 pieces)
5 tbsp. butter
2 tbsp. oil
flour
salt and pepper to taste
3 tbsp. lemon juice
2 tbsp. parsley, minced
2 tbsp. dry white wine
very thin lemon slices

Dredge scaloppine very lightly in flour and shake off the excess. Heat 3 tablespoons butter and the oil in a skillet. When the fats start foaming, add the meat, not too many pieces at a time, brown them quickly on one side, turn and brown the other side. This should take not more than a minute or two.

As they are done, remove them to a warm platter and season with salt and pepper. Take skillet off the flame, add lemon juice and wine, scrape the pan to deglaze. Swirl in the remaining butter, then add parsley, blend and return scaloppine to the sauce. Return skillet to stove, heat through very briefly. Put meat on a hot serving platter, sauce over it and garnish with lemon slices and a little chopped parsley.

Veal Chops in Piquante Sauce

(for 4)

4 veal chops, about 1-inch thick
2 tbsp. flour
2 tbsp. butter
1 tbsp. olive oil
6 anchovy filets, mashed
¼ tsp. basil
½ tsp. sage
salt and pepper to taste
2 tsp. very small capers, well drained
½ cup dry white wine
1 tsp. lemon juice
¼ cup beef broth
1 tsp. beef extract (bovril or similar)

Dust chops lightly with flour and season with salt and pepper. Heat butter and oil in a heavy saucepan and brown chops on both sides. When browned, remove from pan and keep warm.

Add anchovies, basil and sage to pan, stir well and sauté for a couple of minutes, then add capers, wine, lemon juice, beef broth and beef extract, blend well and stir to deglaze pan. Simmer for a few minutes to reduce the liquid by about one quarter. Then return chops to pan, cover and simmer for 20 minutes or until chops are cooked.

Ossobuco

(for 4)

4 meaty pieces of shin of veal, with the bone, about 4 inches long
flour
salt and pepper to taste
3 tbsp. butter
3 tbsp. olive oil
½ cup carrots, minced
½ cup onion, minced
1 large clove garlic, minced
1 tbsp. parsley, chopped
¾ cup dry white wine
¾ cup chicken broth
¼ tsp. thyme
2 strips lemon peel
¼ tsp. rosemary
2 tbsp. tomato paste
½ cup celery, minced

Dredge meat in flour, shake off excess, season with salt and pepper. Heat half the butter and oil in a heavy skillet or dutch oven. Brown the meat on all sides. Remove from pan, which ideally should just be big enough to contain the shank pieces standing upright. Pour off the fat and add the remaining oil and butter. Add all the vegetables, sauté while stirring until they are lightly browned. Add wine and chicken broth, place meat on top of vegetables, add all other ingredients, cover tightly and simmer for about 1½ hours or until meat is done. Baste every 15 minutes. When meat is done remove to hot serving platter, strain the sauce and reduce quickly if too thin.

Saltimbocca Romana

(for 4)

1½ lbs. scallopine
(veal cutlets, cut very thin)
¼ lb. prosciutto
(or lean bacon)
fresh sage leaves (or 1
tsp. dried sage)
2 tbsp. butter
2 tbsp. olive oil
salt and pepper to taste
½ cup chicken broth

Cut the veal cutlets in 4-inch squares. Sprinkle a little sage on each square, put a slice of prosciutto or bacon on top and fasten to veal with a toothpick. Season with salt and pepper. Heat butter and oil in a skillet and brown the meat quickly on both sides. This should not take longer than 2 or 3 minutes. Remove the saltimbocca as they get done to a hot serving platter, then add broth to the skillet, scrape and deglaze the skillet, reduce the gravy if too thin, and pour over meat.

Stuffed Breast of Veal

(for 6)

1 breast of veal
6 tbsp. olive oil
½ cup uncooked rice
2 cups fresh breadcrumbs
lukewarm milk
¼ cup salt pork, finely diced and blanched
½ cup chicken livers
½ cup grated provolone cheese
½ lb. spinach, blanched and finely chopped
2 egg yolks
½ tsp. dried basil
pinch of grated nutmeg
1 large onion, chopped
2 carrots, peeled and chopped
1 leek, white and green part, washed and chopped

Have butcher bone the veal for stuffing and give you the bones as well as the meat.

Heat 1 tablespoon oil in a casserole, add the rice and stir until the rice becomes translucent. Add ¾ cup of water and a little salt. Cover tightly and cook for about 17 minutes or until rice is tender.

Soak the breadcrumbs in lukewarm milk. Squeeze them dry. Mince together the salt pork and the chicken livers. Mix them with the cooked rice, the breadcrumbs, spinach, grated cheese, egg yolks and basil. Season with salt, pepper and nutmeg. Stuff the breast of veal with this mixture and sew the opening closed.

Put the chopped vegetables in a casserole with the remaining oil and veal bones. Place the stuffed breast of veal on top and cook over high heat for 7 or 8 minutes. Turn the meat and cook it on the other side for 7 or 8 minutes. Cover the casserole and transfer it to a preheated 350° oven. Bake for about 2½ hours. After 1 hour cooking time, pierce the meat in three places with a needle. Baste occasionally.

Drain the cooked meat, place it on a large serving dish. Skim the fat off the pan juices and strain the juices over the meat. Chill until serving time. Serve cold, garnished with tomato slices and black olives.

VINTAGE 1970
VINTAGE 1970
IMPORTED
SOAVE
IMPORTED
ALPOLICELLA
CLASSICO SUPERIORE
UFFINO

Scaloppine Marsala

(for 4)

12 thin small veal scaloppine
salt and pepper to taste
flour
4 tbsp. butter
1 tbsp. oil
½ cup dry marsala wine
¼ cup chicken broth

Season veal with salt and pepper, dredge lightly in flour. Heat butter and oil in a skillet, sauté scaloppine gently until brown on both sides and meat is cooked. Remove from skillet and keep warm. Add 1 tablespoon flour to skillet, stir for a minute, add wine and stir well to deglaze the skillet, add broth, mix and cook rapidly until sauce thickens. Pour over meat and serve.

←*Stuffed Breast of Veal.*

←*Spaghetti Carbonara. See page 43 for recipe.*

Veal Cutlets Milanese

(for 4)

1½ lbs. veal scalloppine
2 eggs, lightly beaten
with 1 tbsp. milk
1½ cups (approx.) fine
white dry breadcrumbs,
unflavored
6 tbsp. butter
2 tbsp. olive oil
salt
lemon wedges

Have veal cut about ¼ inch thick and then well flattened. Dip each cutlet in beaten eggs, then in breadcrumbs. Press crumbs gently with your hands into the meat, then shake off excess crumbs. Letting the cutlets rest after breading will make the breading adhere better.

Heat butter and oil in a skillet. The fats should be about ¼ inch deep. Cook the cutlets over medium heat until golden brown, turn when one side is done. Drain on paper towel, sprinkle with salt and serve garnished with lemon wedges.

Veal Cutlets with Parmesan

Proceed as for veal cutlets Milanese, but mix ¼ cup parmesan cheese with the breadcrumbs before breading the meat.

Veal and Peppers

(for 4)

2 tbsp. butter
1 tbsp. oil
1½ lbs. boneless veal
(shoulder or rump) cubed
salt and pepper to taste
1 medium onion,
sliced thin

4 firm ripe tomatoes,
peeled, seeded and chopped
1 tsp. dried basil, crumbled
½ tsp. marjoram
4 large sweet peppers
(green or red or mixed)
3 tbsp. olive oil

Heat butter and oil in a saucepan, add veal cubes and brown. Season with salt and pepper, add onion, stir well and cook over medium heat for 5 minutes. Add tomatoes, basil and marjoram, mix well, cover and simmer for 20 minutes. Cut caps off peppers and discard. Remove seeds and membranes; quarter peppers lengthwise. Heat olive oil in a skillet and fry peppers for 5 minutes or more until soft. Then add to the veal, cover again and simmer another half hour or until meat is cooked. Correct seasoning before serving.

Veal and Tuna Sauce

(for 8 to 10)

3 lbs. boneless veal (shoulder or leg)
2 stalks celery
2 carrots
2 bay leaves
4 sprigs parsley
1 onion stuck with 1 clove
pinch of thyme
chicken broth
salt and pepper to taste
1 can (7 oz.) tuna canned in olive oil
1 can anchovy filets with the oil
½ cup olive oil
2 tbsp. lemon juice
1 tbsp. capers
1 tbsp. parsley, minced

Have butcher roll and tie the veal. Place veal in a saucepan, cover with half water and half chicken broth. Add celery, carrots, bay leaves, parsley, onion, thyme, salt and pepper, and bring to a boil. Cover and cook gently for about 1½ hours or until meat is tender. Cool in the broth and then drain.

Put tuna with its oil, anchovies and their oil in a food processor or blender. Process and add gradually olive oil and lemon juice and blend until the sauce is very smooth and creamy.

Slice the veal very thin, put in a glass or ceramic dish, pour the sauce over it and refrigerate overnight. Before serving sprinkle with capers and parsley.

Veal Stew with Wine

(for 4)

1½ lbs. boneless veal (shoulder or shank) cubed
2 tbsp. shallots, minced
3 tbsp. butter
1 tbsp. olive oil
flour
¾ cup dry white wine
½ tsp. rosemary
½ tsp. sage
pinch of grated nutmeg
½ tsp. grated lemon rind
salt and pepper to taste
2 tbsp. parsley, chopped

Heat oil and butter in a saucepan, sauté shallots until soft but not browned. Dredge veal cubes in flour, add to pan, a few at a time, and sauté until well browned. Remove browned pieces to a warm platter before cooking the next ones. When all the meat has been browned, add wine to saucepan, scrape to deglaze and dissolve the brown particles; add rosemary, sage, nutmeg and lemon rind, season with salt and pepper and return meat to pan. Cover and cook over gentle heat for about 1 hour or until meat is done. Stir once in a while. A few minutes before serving, sprinkle with chopped parsley.

Beefsteak Pizzaiola

(for 2)

1 porterhouse steak, about 2 inches thick
2 tbsp. olive oil
salt and pepper to taste
2 cloves garlic, minced
1 cup canned tomatoes, drained and chopped
½ tsp. rosemary
1 tsp. oregano
¼ cup dry red wine

Trim the steak. Heat oil in a heavy skillet, panbroil steak to taste. Sprinkle with salt and pepper. Remove from skillet and keep warm. Pour off all fat but 1 tablespoon. Add garlic to skillet, sauté for one minute, add tomatoes, herbs and wine, blend well and cook over high heat for about 2 minutes until slightly reduced. Pour sauce over steak when serving.

Stuffed Beef Rolls

(Bracioli)

(for 4)

4 thin slices of round steak
4 slices prosciutto ham
½ cup fresh white breadcrumbs
⅓ cup grated romano
1 cup beef broth
2 cloves garlic, minced
salt and pepper to taste
4 tbsp. olive oil
2 cups canned Italian tomatoes, drained and chopped
2 tbsp. tomato paste
½ cup dry red wine
½ tsp. oregano
4 tbsp. parsley, minced

Have butcher pound the slices of steak; they should be quite thin. Blend breadcrumbs, cheese, garlic, parsley, oregano, and season with salt and pepper. Place a slice of prosciutto on top of each steak, then spread one fourth of the breadcrumb mixture in the center of each slice, roll it up, tuck in the ends and tie with thread.

Heat olive oil in a heavy casserole, brown the meat rolls on all sides. Add tomatoes, tomato paste, wine and half a cup of broth, bring to a boil, cover and simmer for about 1½ hours. Add more broth if necessary. When meat is tender, season sauce with salt and pepper and serve.

Pot Roast Triestine

(for 6 to 8)

2 tbsp. olive oil
1 beef round, boneless rump roast, about 4 lbs.
2 large onions, sliced thin
2 cloves garlic, minced
1½ cups beef broth
salt and pepper to taste
1 cup dry red wine
1 bay leaf
½ tsp. thyme
1 tsp. oregano
2 anchovy filets, mashed
1 strip orange peel (2" x 1")
1½ lbs. carrots, peeled and cut in 2-inch pieces

Heat olive oil in a dutch oven or heavy casserole, add meat and brown on all sides. Remove meat from pan. To drippings add onions and garlic and sauté until lightly browned. Drain off fat. Return roast to pan, add wine, broth, salt, pepper, bay leaf, thyme, oregano, anchovy and orange peel. Cover and simmer 2 hours, turning meat once. Add carrots and cook 45 minutes or until carrots and meat are tender.

Remove meat to serving platter and keep hot. Remove carrots with a slotted spoon and put around meat. Skim fat off sauce and reduce quickly to desired consistency. Remove bay leaf and orange peel, correct seasoning and serve gravy with the pot roast.

Beef Stew Roman Style

(for 4)

2½ lbs. lean beef
(chuck or shoulder)
2 cups canned tomatoes
½ cup celery, chopped
1 medium onion, chopped
1 carrot, chopped
5 sprigs parsley
1 bay leaf
1 tsp. rosemary
½ tsp. marjoram
2 tbsp. olive oil
2 cloves garlic, minced
1 cup dry white wine
salt and pepper to taste

Cut meat in 1 inch cubes. Put tomatoes, celery, onion, carrot, parsley, bay leaf, rosemary and marjoram in a saucepan, cover and cook gently for about half an hour. Force through a fine sieve and reserve sauce.

Heat oil in another casserole, brown meat cubes quickly, add garlic, stir and add the tomato sauce, wine, salt and pepper. Cover and simmer for about 1½ hours or until meat is tender. Remove meat with a slotted spoon, keep warm. Reduce sauce by about one third, return meat, adjust seasoning and heat through. Serve with garlic bread.

Aromatic Pork Chops

(for 4)

4 loin pork chops
(about 1¼ inches thick)
2 tbsp. butter
salt and pepper to taste
1 tbsp. grated onion
1 tbsp. tomato paste
½ cup dry white wine
¼ cup sherry
1 small clove garlic, crushed
½ tsp. marjoram
1 tbsp. lemon juice
1½ tbsp. anisette or other
anise flavored cordial

Trim most of the fat off the chops. Heat butter in a skillet and sauté chops for about 15 minutes on each side over gentle heat, until well cooked. Remove to hot serving platter. Add all other ingredients except anisette to skillet, scrape and deglaze the pan, let come to a boil and cook over moderate heat for 5 minutes until well blended and slightly thickened. Correct seasoning. Add anisette, blend, simmer for 1 minute, then pour sauce over chops and serve.

Braised Pork Chops

(for 4)

2 tbsp. butter
4 loin pork chops
(about 1 inch thick)
salt and pepper to taste
½ cup dry vermouth
(or white wine)

½ tsp. grated lemon rind
1 tbsp. grated onion
½ tsp. rosemary, crushed
½ tsp. sage
1½ tbsp. lemon juice
1 tbsp. parsley, chopped

Trim most of the fat off the chops. Heat butter in a saucepan, brown chops on both sides. Season with salt and pepper, add vermouth, lemon rind, onion, rosemary and sage. Cover and cook gently for about 30 minutes or until meat is tender. Turn chops once during cooking. Just before serving, remove chops to hot serving platter, stir lemon juice and parsley into the pan gravy, reduce quickly if necessary and pour over chops.

Stuffed Pork Chops

(for 4)

4 loin pork chops, 1¼ inch thick
4 thin slices mozarella cheese
4 slices capocollo (or Canadian bacon) cut in strips
2 tbsp. brandy (opt.)
1 egg, lightly beaten with 1 tbsp. milk
½ cup fine dry bread-crumbs (unseasoned)
3 tbsp. oil
2 tbsp. butter
salt and pepper to taste

Have butcher cut a pocket in each chop and trim off most of the fat. Put a slice of cheese in each pocket, also a few strips of capocollo, and sprinkle some brandy in each pocket. Close pockets with a toothpick. Season chops with salt and pepper. Dip in beaten egg and roll in bread-crumbs. Shake off excess crumbs. Heat oil and butter in a skillet and fry chops for 15 to 20 minutes on each side.

Braised Leg of Lamb

(for 4)

½ leg of lamb
(about 3 lbs.)
1 cup dry white wine
¼ cup onion, chopped
¼ cup carrot, chopped
¼ cup celery, chopped
2 cloves garlic, crushed
½ tsp. rosemary, crushed
1 tbsp. juniper berries
1 anchovy filet, mashed
salt and pepper to taste
2 tbsp. brandy

Trim most of the fat off the lamb. Place lamb in a heavy casserole or dutch oven, add all ingredients except brandy, cover tightly and cook gently for about 1½ hours. Turn several times while cooking. Then remove lid to allow some steam to escape and cook another 1½ hours. The meat should be quite tender. Remove meat from pot, skim off fat and reduce sauce quickly. The sauce should be rich and creamy. Return meat to sauce, heat through, pour brandy over it, flame and serve.

Italian Spring Lamb

(for 6)

1 leg of lamb, about 6 lbs.
salt and pepper
2 cloves garlic, mashed
1/3 cup dry red wine
2 tbsp. chopped fresh basil or 2 tsp. dried basil
2 tbsp. grated parmesan cheese
1/3 cup olive oil

Sprinkle lamb on all sides with salt and pepper. Place lamb in a shallow roasting pan. Beat remaining ingredients in a bowl until thick and well blended. Brush some of the wine mixture over lamb. Roast in a preheated oven at 350° for about 1¾ hours for pink lamb and 2½ hours for well-done lamb. Brush lamb with wine mixture every 30 minutes during cooking. Garnish with additional sprigs of fresh basil if desired. Allow cooked lamb to stand 10 minutes before carving.

Serve garnished with a vegetable medley of cooked zucchini slices and onions, artichoke hearts and roasted red pepper pieces if desired.

Sautéed Liver Venetian Style

(for 4)

1½ lbs. calf liver, very thinly sliced
2 Bermuda onions, thinly sliced
4 tbsp. oil
1 tbsp. butter
salt and pepper to taste

Trim liver, remove skin or gristle and cut into bite size strips. Heat oil and butter in a large skillet, sauté onion slices gently for about 15 minutes until soft and golden brown. Stir occasionally. Remove onion from skillet with a slotted spoon, leaving all the fat in the skillet. Turn up the flame, and when fat is hot, add the liver and sauté very quickly while stirring, just long enough for liver to be seared and turning brownish. Sprinkle with salt and pepper, return onions to skillet, stir, heat through, serve immediately.

Rice

Rice is a very important staple in Italian cooking, and the way of preparing *risotto,* the uniquely Italian rice dish, is quite different from other methods of cooking rice. A risotto is not a rice pilaff, nor a plain cooked rice in the European or Far Eastern manner. A real risotto has a soft, creamy texture, even though the rice grains retain their shape, and are still firm to the bite and not mushy.

The variety of risotto dishes is endless — almost all kinds of food (seafood, meat, poultry, vegetables) can be combined with the rice. The best kind of rice to use is the short, stubby Italian rice, available in many food stores. A good long grain rice is a fair substitute for Italian rice, though the texture will be different. Do not use precooked or "instant rice."

Italian Spring Lamb. See page 106 for recipe. →

VINTAGE
1970
IMPORTED
LUGANA
RUFFINO
IMPORTED
BARDOLINO
CLASSICO SUPERIORE
RUFFINO

Basic Risotto and Cheese

(for 4 to 6)

6 cups chicken broth
5 tbsp. butter
2 tbsp. onion, minced
1 small clove garlic, minced
1½ cups uncooked rice
¼ tsp. saffron
½ cup grated parmesan cheese
salt and pepper to taste

Heat the chicken broth and keep it simmering. Heat 4 tablespoons butter in a heavy saucepan, add onions and garlic and sauté until onion is transparent and limp. Do not let brown. Add the raw, unwashed rice and stir until rice is well coated with butter and translucent. Add ½ cup hot broth and cook while stirring until the liquid is absorbed. Then add another half cup of liquid, keep stirring; when that has been absorbed, add more and continue cooking while stirring, taking care that no rice sticks to the bottom of the pan. After using 2 or 3 cups, add saffron to remaining broth, season with salt and pepper and continue the cooking procedure as above, until the rice is cooked but still firm. About 20 to 25 minutes should do it. There might be some broth left over — the exact quantities of broth needed for a risotto are hard to measure; it depends on the quality of the rice, cooking temperature, etc.

About 5 minutes before the rice is ready to be served, add the remaining tablespoon of butter and the cheese, blend well and finish cooking. The risotto should be creamy but not liquid.

←*Spaghetti with Mussels. See page 51 for recipe.*

Risotto Milanese

(for 6)

6 cups chicken broth
6 tbsp. butter
2 tbsp. minced onion
2 tbsp. beef marrow (opt.)

1½ cups rice
¾ cup dry white wine
¼ tsp. saffron threads
salt and pepper to taste
⅔ cup parmesan cheese, grated

Heat chicken broth and keep simmering. Combine saffron with a little hot chicken broth and reserve. Heat 3 tablespoons butter in a heavy saucepan, add onion and diced beef marrow and sauté until onion is limp and translucent. Add rice and stir until rice is well coated with butter and translucent. Add wine and saffron; cook and stir until liquid is nearly absorbed, then continue cooking as for Basic Risotto *(p.)*. When rice is nearly done, stir in remaining butter and the grated cheese and finish cooking.

Rice and Chicken Livers

(for 6)

Note: This is not a risotto of the Milanese style, but rice cooked in the way pilafs are prepared. The name "risotto" can be somewhat confusing, since in some parts of Italy any rice dish is called a risotto.

4 tbsp. butter
½ lb. chicken livers
3 tbsp. onion, minced
½ cup chopped mushrooms
1 small clove garlic, minced
2 tbsp. parsley, chopped
1½ cups rice
3½ cups chicken broth
salt and pepper to taste
grated parmesan cheese

Trim chicken livers and cut in half. Heat butter in a heavy saucepan, add livers and sauté quickly until browned but still pink inside. Remove livers and keep warm. Add onion and garlic to saucepan, sauté until onion is limp, add mushrooms and parsley, blend and cook for a minute. Add rice, and sauté while stirring for 2 minutes. Do not let rice brown. Add chicken broth, salt and pepper, blend, cover the pan and bring to a boil. Lower heat and cook for 20 minutes or until rice is cooked. Stir once with a fork during cooking. When rice is cooked, stir in the chicken livers and serve with the cheese on the side.

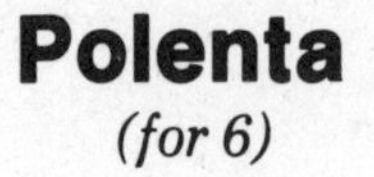

Polenta

(for 6)

1½ cups cornmeal
5 cups water
1 tbsp. salt

Bring water to boil in a heavy saucepan or kettle. Add salt, turn the heat down so that the water is just simmering. Add the cornmeal gradually in a thin stream while stirring with a wooden spoon. Keep stirring constantly and be sure that the water stays at the simmering point.

After all the cornmeal has been added to the water, keep stirring and simmering for about 15 to 30 minutes until the mixture is so thick that the spoon will stand up in the middle and the mixture comes away from the sides of pot when stirred.

Pour polenta into a serving platter.

In the north of Italy, especially in Lombardy and in the Northeast, polenta is the essential everyday dish and has been so for generations. In most farmhouses and homes it is made fresh every day — prepared in copper kettles. It is often served as a first course — like rice or spaghetti dishes, or served with meat or game.

Polenta Cacciatore

(for 6)

1½ lbs. veal (shoulder or rump) cut in 1 inch cubes
1 tbsp. butter
1 tbsp. oil
½ cup minced onion
1 clove garlic, minced
3 cups canned Italian tomatoes, chopped
½ cup dry white wine
1 tsp. dried basil
salt and pepper to taste
1 recipe polenta *(p. 114)*

Heat butter and oil in a heavy saucepan, add onion, garlic and meat and sauté until browned. Add tomatoes, wine, basil, salt and pepper, cover and cook for about 45 minutes or until meat is tender.

Put hot polenta on a serving platter, cover with the veal and sauce and serve.

Polenta with Sausage

(for 6)

1½ lbs. Italian sausage (sweet or hot or mixed)
3 tbsp. dry white wine
¼ cup chopped onion
1 clove garlic, minced
2 cups canned Italian tomatoes, chopped
1 cup tomato puree
¾ cup dry white wine
1 pinch of thyme
salt and pepper to taste
1 recipe polenta *(p. 114)*
¼ cup grated parmesan cheese

Prick sausage with a needle, place in a saucepan, add 3 tablespoons wine and sauté until wine has evaporated and sausages are browned. Add onion, garlic and sauté another 2 minutes. Add tomatoes, white wine, tomato puree, thyme, salt and pepper and simmer for 1½ hours. Put hot polenta on a serving dish, pour sausages and gravy over it, sprinkle with grated cheese and serve.

Asparagus Milanese

(for 4)

2 lbs. fresh asparagus
salt and white pepper
  to taste
4 to 5 tbsp. butter
1 tbsp. lemon juice
¾ cup grated parmesan cheese

Trim asparagus, snap off tough ends, peel and tie in bundles. Fill a narrow high pan with enough water to cover two thirds of the bundled asparagus, but leave the upper third and tips out of the water. Bring water to a boil, add asparagus and cover. Cook for 10 to 15 minutes, depending on the thickness of the stalks, until the tip of a knife pierces the stalks easily. Do not overcook. Drain and cool the cooked stalks.

Butter the bottom of an oblong baking dish, place a row of asparagus in the dish, sprinkle with salt, pepper, parmesan and dot with butter. Cover this layer with another row of asparagus, arrange the tips to face away from those in the bottom row. Sprinkle again with salt, pepper, parmesan, dot with butter. Repeat until all asparagus have been used. Sprinkle top layer with a good amount of cheese, dot with butter and sprinkle with lemon juice. Bake in 425° oven for about 15 minutes until top is golden brown.

Fried Asparagus

(for 4)

1½ lbs. fresh asparagus
    (medium thick stalks)
2 eggs, beaten with
  2 tbsp. milk

vegetable oil for frying
salt to taste
lemon wedges
fine dry white breadcrumbs

Snap off tough ends of asparagus, wash well, trim off scales and cut to uniform length.

Put oil in a heavy skillet to about ½ inch depth. Heat oil, dip asparagus in beaten egg, then roll in breadcrumbs. Place a few stalks at a time in hot oil and fry until golden brown on one side. Turn and fry the other side. Remove and drain on paper towel and salt to taste. Repeat until all asparagus have been fried. Serve with lemon wedges.

Green Beans

(for 4)

1½ lbs. young crisp green beans
⅔ cup thinly sliced onion
1 clove garlic, minced
1 medium green pepper, seeded and cut into narrow strips
¾ cup canned Italian tomatoes with their juice, chopped
½ cup chicken broth
1 tsp. lemon juice
salt and pepper to taste
4 tbsp. olive oil

Heat oil in a saucepan, add onion and garlic and sauté until onion is soft. Add the pepper and tomatoes and cook uncovered over gentle heat for about 20 minutes. Stir once in a while. When the tomatoes have cooked down to a thick sauce, add the beans, stir well, add salt, pepper, chicken broth and lemon juice, cover and cook quickly until beans are done, 12 to 20 minutes, depending on their size.

Three Bean Salad

(for 6)

1 can chick peas, drained
1 can lima beans, drained
1 can kidney beans, drained
1 small onion, minced
1/3 cup canned pimento, diced
3 scallions, chopped
2 anchovy filets, mashed
1 clove garlic, mashed
salt and pepper to taste
½ tsp. oregano
½ tsp. basil
1 tbsp. parsley, minced
5 tbsp. olive oil
1½ tbsp. vinegar

Put peas, beans, onion, pimento and scallions in a bowl. Blend all other ingredients, pour over vegetables and mix well. Let stand for an hour or so before serving.

Broccoli Palermo

(for 4)

1 bunch broccoli
¼ cup olive oil
1 Bermuda onion, sliced thin
1 sweet red pepper, seeded and cut into narrow strips
½ cup minced prosciutto ham
½ cup provolone cheese, diced fine
salt and pepper to taste
⅔ cup dry white wine
12 pimento-stuffed green olives, sliced

Wash broccoli and trim off coarse stems. Put in a bowl, pour boiling water over broccoli, let stand for 2 minutes, drain and cool. Cut broccoli in thin slices.

Put one tablespoon olive oil in a saucepan, cover the bottom of the pan with a thin layer of sliced onions, a few sliced olives and a sprinkle of prosciutto. Then add a layer of broccoli, season with salt and pepper, sprinkle with oil and diced cheese. Repeat until all ingredients have been used up. Place pepper strips on top, pour remaining oil over the top; add the wine, cover and cook gently for about half an hour until broccoli is done.

Broccoli Medici

(for 4)

1 large bunch broccoli
1 cup mayonnaise (approx.)
salt and pepper to taste
1 tsp. lemon juice
⅛ tsp. grated nutmeg

Cut florets off broccoli, discard stems. Wash florets, put them in a bowl. Pour boiling water over them, let stand 1 minute, and drain. Cook florets in boiling salted water for about 10 minutes or until tender. Drain well and chop very fine. While still warm season with salt and pepper, blend with mayonnaise — about ¼ cup mayonnaise for each cup of broccoli — blend in lemon juice and nutmeg and serve. If not hot enough, heat through in a double boiler.

Fried Cauliflower

(for 4)

1 head cauliflower
2 eggs beaten with
  2 tbsp. milk
vegetable oil for frying
fine dry white breadcrumbs
salt to taste
lemon wedges

Trim cauliflower and boil in salted water until just cooked, but still firm (about 20 minutes). Remove from fire, cook and cut off florets, trim to uniform size. Then proceed to cook as in fried asparagus *(p. 118)*.

Eggplant Parmigiana

(for 4)

2 medium eggplants
¾ cup olive oil
2 eggs beaten with
2 tbsp. milk
2 cups fine dry white
breadcrumbs
1½ cups tomato sauce
(p. 146)

1 tsp. basil
½ tsp. oregano
4 tbsp. grated parmesan cheese
½ lb. mozarella cheese,
thinly sliced
salt and pepper to taste

Combine ²/₃ cup breadcrumbs with basil, oregano and parmesan and reserve. Slice eggplants about ½ inch thick. Dip in beaten egg and coat with unflavored breadcrumbs. Fry slices in hot oil until browned on both sides. Remove from pan, drain on paper towel. Place a layer of slices in the bottom of a baking dish, spread tomato sauce over it, season with salt and pepper and sprinkle with the breadcrumb-cheese mixture. Repeat until all eggplant slices have been used. Cover top with tomato sauce and sliced mozarella and bake in 400° oven for about 15 minutes until cheese has melted and is bubbly.

Eggplant Casserole

(for 4)

2 small eggplants
½ lb. ground beef
1 small onion, minced
1 clove garlic, minced
¾ cup olive oil
1½ cups tomato sauce *(p. 146)*
½ cup romano cheese
1 egg beaten with
2 tbsp. romano cheese
salt and pepper to taste

Heat 2 tablespoons oil, sauté onions and garlic until limp. Add meat and sauté until lightly browned. Reserve and keep warm. Peel eggplant, slice ¼ inch thick and fry in oil until golden brown, drain on paper towel. Blend tomato sauce with cheese.

Place a layer of fried eggplant in the bottom of a casserole. Put some of the fried meat on top, coat with tomato-cheese mixture. Season with salt and pepper. Repeat until all ingredients have been used up. Pour egg mixture over the top layer and bake in 400° oven for about 20 minutes.

Fennel (Finocchio) au Gratin

(for 6)

4 fresh fennel bulbs, trimmed and quartered
3 tbsp. butter
3 tbsp. flour
2 cups hot milk
salt and white pepper to taste
pinch of grated nutmeg
small pinch cayenne pepper (opt.)
4 tbsp. grated parmesan
2 egg yolks, beaten
2 tbsp. butter

Cook fennel in boiling salted water for about 8 minutes. Drain and reserve. Melt 3 tablespoons butter in a small saucepan, stir in flour, and cook stirring until mixture bubbles — do not let brown. Add slowly, while stirring, hot milk, salt, pepper, nutmeg and cayenne; stir or whisk until mixture is smooth and thickened; stir in two tablespoons parmesan, blend well. Remove from fire, blend in egg yolks, correct seasoning. Return to very gentle fire and heat through while stirring for a minute or two. Arrange fennel in a well buttered baking dish, cover with sauce and sprinkle with remaining parmesan. Bake in 400° oven for 10 to 15 minutes until top is golden brown.

Mushrooms Marinara

(for 6)

1 lb. fresh mushrooms, sliced
3 cups fresh tomatoes, peeled, seeded and chopped
¾ cup thinly sliced onion
2 tbsp. olive oil
½ tsp. oregano
½ tsp. lemon juice
salt and pepper to taste
1 clove garlic, minced

Heat oil in a saucepan, sauté onion and garlic until soft but not browned. Add tomatoes, oregano, salt, pepper and lemon juice and cook uncovered until liquid has been reduced and the tomatoes have become pulpy. Add sliced mushrooms to tomato sauce and simmer 8 to 10 minutes or until mushrooms are just tender.

Braised Green Onions

(for 4)

12 large new onions (or large white onions if not available)
2 tbsp. oil
½ cup dry red wine
salt and pepper to taste
2 tbsp. sugar

Put oil in a heavy saucepan just large enough to contain the onions in one layer. Skin and pare onions, and place in pan. Start to cook uncovered over medium heat until oil sizzles, then add wine, sugar, salt and pepper and enough water to cover the bottom of the pan about 1 inch deep with liquids.

Cover and cook over medium heat adding a little more water as needed. During cooking turn onions quite frequently with a spoon. Cook for about two hours. The onions will be soft and the liquid in the pan syrupy and quite brown.

Stuffed Tomatoes

(for 4)

4 large, ripe, firm tomatoes
2 tbsp. olive oil
¼ cup onion, chopped
4 anchovy filets, mashed
6 pitted green olives, minced
2 tbsp. olive oil
⅔ cup soft white breadcrumbs
1 tbsp. parsley
salt and pepper to taste
2 tbsp. fine dry breadcrumbs

Cut tops off tomatoes and scoop out pulp. Heat olive oil in a skillet, sauté onion until light golden. Remove from fire and blend with anchovy, olives, soft breadcrumbs, parsley and season with salt and pepper. Stuff the tomato shells, sprinkle the top with dry breadcrumbs and olive oil. Put tomatoes in an oiled baking dish and bake at 375° for about half an hour.

Peas and Prosciutto

(for 4)

3 tbsp. butter
1/3 cup thinly sliced onion
2 cups green peas
½ cup prosciutto ham, chopped
¼ cup chicken broth
salt and pepper to taste
½ tsp. sugar
1½ tbsp. parsley, chopped

Heat butter in a saucepan, add onion and sauté gently until onion is soft and just starts to color. Add peas, chicken broth, salt, pepper and sugar; cook for 10 minutes, then stir in prosciutto and parsley and cook until peas are tender.

Braised Peppers

(for 4)

4 large green peppers
1 medium onion, sliced thin
1 tbsp. butter
1 tbsp. olive oil
3 tbsp. dry white wine
2 large ripe tomatoes, peeled and coarsely chopped
salt and pepper to taste
1 tbsp. parsley, chopped
½ tsp. lemon juice

Seed peppers and cut into narrow rings. Heat oil and butter in a saucepan, sauté onion until light golden in color. Add tomatoes, blend and simmer for 5 minutes. Add green peppers, salt, pepper, parsley, lemon juice and wine, cover and cook gently for about half an hour. Stir frequently to avoid sticking and add a little more wine if necessary.

Parmesan Potatoes

(for 4)

4 large potatoes, peeled and diced small
2 tbsp. butter
1 tbsp. beef extract (bovril or other)
3 tbsp. water
salt and pepper to taste
pinch of grated nutmeg
pinch of thyme
1/3 cup beef broth
4 tbsp. melted butter
½ cup grated parmesan cheese

Heat 2 tablespoons butter in a saucepan, add potatoes, stir well, cover and cook for about 10 to 15 minutes, until just soft. Blend beef extract with water, add to potatoes; also broth, salt, pepper, nutmeg and thyme; blend well. Put potatoes in a buttered baking dish, cover top with melted butter, sprinkle with parmesan and bake at 425° for about 12 minutes until top is golden brown.

Mashed Potatoes Milanese

(for 4)

4 cups boiled potatoes
5 tbsp. butter
1/3 cup milk
2/3 cup grated parmesan cheese
salt and pepper to taste

Mash hot potatoes, add butter and milk, whisk until they are quite fluffy. Add salt and pepper and ½ cup of parmesan. Whisk until well mixed. Put mixture in a buttered gratin or soufflé dish. Do not fill to the top since the potatoes will fluff up during baking. Sprinkle top with remaining cheese and bake in 375° oven for about 15 minutes until nicely browned.

Spinach Florentine

(for 4)

2 lbs. spinach
4 anchovy filets
4 tbsp. butter, melted
4 eggs
$^1/_3$ cup romano cheese, grated
3 tbsp. fine dry white breadcrumbs
pinch of grated nutmeg
1 clove garlic, mashed with salt
pepper to taste

Wash spinach, trim off coarse stalks and cook. Drain well and chop. Butter 4 small baking dishes or ramekins, put one fourth of the spinach in each. Cover each portion with an anchovy filet, sprinkle with melted butter, make a slight hollow with the back of a spoon and put a raw egg in it. Blend all other ingredients, sprinkle over eggs and bake in 400° oven for about 15 minutes until eggs are set.

Zucchini Casserole

(for 4)

1½ lbs. medium zucchini
½ cup olive oil
1 medium onion, thinly sliced
2 cloves garlic, minced
½ cup celery, white part, diced
¾ cup canned Italian tomatoes with their juice, chopped
2 tbsp. parsley, chopped
¼ tsp. marjoram
salt and pepper to taste
1 tbsp. fresh lemon juice

Clean zucchini, pare off ends, and slice them crosswise about ½ inch thick. Heat olive oil in a flame proof dish or serving casserole, add onion and garlic and sauté until limp and just starting to color. Add tomatoes and their juice, celery, lemon juice, parsley, marjoram; stir and simmer for about 15 minutes. Add zucchini, blend, correct seasoning and bake at 350° for about 30 minutes or until zucchini are cooked but still firm.

Cabbage Cacciatore

(for 6)

1½ lbs. lean ground beef
1 cup onions, chopped
1 cup celery, chopped
1½ tsp. salt
pepper to taste
1 tsp. paprika
1 clove garlic, crushed
1 medium head cabbage (about 1½ lbs.) cut into 6 wedges
2 cups canned tomato sauce
½ tsp. basil
½ tsp. oregano
1 cup grated mozarella cheese
3 cups hot cooked rice

In an ovenproof skillet sauté beef, onions, celery, salt, pepper, paprika and garlic until meat is no longer pink and vegetables are tender crisp, stirring frequently to crumble meat. Arrange cabbage wedges on top of meat mixture.

Blend tomato sauce, basil, oregano, pour over cabbage wedges. Cover tightly and bake at 350° for 45 minutes or until cabbage is tender. Remove cover; sprinkle with cheese, return to oven for 5 minutes. Serve over bed of rice.

Cabbage Cacciatora.→

Fried Zucchini

(for 4)

1 lb. medium zucchini
salt and white pepper
oil for frying
1 cup flour
white wine vinegar
parsley

Scrub zucchini well, rub with a towel, cut off ends. Cut them into sticks of uniform length, about ¼ inch thick, sprinkle with salt and pepper and let stand for half an hour. Drain, pat dry with paper towels.

Put oil in a heavy skillet to about ½ inch depth and heat. Dredge zucchini sticks lightly in flour, shake off excess and fry, a few at a time, in hot oil until browned on all sides. Put on paper towels to drain and sprinkle while still hot with a few drops of vinegar and salt to taste.

Garnish with parsley when serving.

←*Bowl of Fruit.*

Green Bean and Onion Salad

(for 6)

1 lb. fresh green beans
½ cup white onions, sliced paper thin
¼ cup green pepper, diced
1 tbsp. parsley, chopped
½ tsp. oregano
½ tsp. basil
salt and pepper to taste
5 tbsp. olive oil
1½ tbsp. wine vinegar

Trim beans, cook in salted water, uncovered, for about 6 minutes. Add onions and cook until beans are barely tender. Drain, blend all other ingredients, add to beans and onions, toss and serve warm or chilled.

Broccoli Salad

(for 6)

2 small bunches broccoli
½ cup mayonnaise
1 tbsp. lemon juice
1 tsp. dried basil
1 tbsp. canned pimento, chopped
1 small tomato, peeled, seeded and chopped
salt and pepper to taste

Trim broccoli and discard tough stems. Cook in boiling salted water until just tender. Separate florets and slice tender stalk. Blend all other ingredients and mix with broccoli.

Italian Potato Salad

(for 4)

2 lbs. potatoes
1 cup onion, minced
salt and pepper to taste
3 filets of anchovy, mashed
¼ cup canned pimento, chopped
2 tbsp. parsley, minced
1 tbsp. fresh basil leaves, chopped
4 tbsp. olive oil
3 tbsp. dry white wine
3 tbsp. white wine vinegar

Boil potatoes in their jackets until cooked but still firm. Peel and slice ½ inch thick. Combine all other ingredients, blend well and mix with sliced potatoes.

Tomato Salad

(for 6)

4 firm ripe tomatoes, peeled
1½ tbsp. grated onion
1½ tbsp. salt
4 tbsp. olive oil
1½ tbsp. wine vinegar
1½ tbsp. parsley, minced
pepper to taste

Slice tomatoes about ½ inch thick. Put slices in a bowl, sprinkle with salt, mix in onion, and let stand for an hour or so. Then drain off liquid, blend oil, vinegar, parsley and pepper, pour over tomato slices, mix gently and serve.

Butter and Parmesan Sauce

(4 servings)

½ cup butter (1 stick)
4 tbsp. heavy cream
½ cup grated parmesan cheese
salt and white pepper to taste

Soften butter and beat with a whisk or electric mixer until light and creamy. Then whisk in the cream and, a little at a time, the grated cheese. Season with salt and pepper.

Gorgonzola Sauce

(for 6 servings)

¼ lb. gorgonzola cheese (blue cheese can be used instead)
½ cup light cream
4 tbsp. dry white wine
salt and pepper to taste
1 tbsp. parsley, minced
2 tbsp. butter

Put cheese, cream, butter, salt and pepper into a saucepan. Heat over a low flame and mash cheese to blend with cream. When well blended, add wine and parsley to the sauce and heat through before serving over spaghetti or noodles. Sprinkle noodles with grated parmesan before serving.

Ragu Bolognese
Meat Sauce

3 tbsp. olive oil
3 tbsp. butter
3 tbsp. minced onion
1 small clove garlic, minced
3 tbsp. celery, white part only, minced
1 carrot, peeled and minced
½ lb. beef (chuck) ground
½ lb. lean pork, ground
salt and pepper to taste
1 cup dry white wine
2 cups canned Italian tomatoes, mashed
½ cup chicken broth
1 cup sliced mushrooms

Heat oil and butter in a heavy saucepan, add onion and garlic, sauté until soft but not browned. Add celery and carrot and sauté 2 or 3 more minutes, stirring occasionally. Add meats, stir well to break up lumps and sauté for 3 or 4 minutes, season with salt and pepper, add wine and tomatoes, blend and simmer for an hour. Add mushrooms and chicken broth and simmer for another hour or so. Stir occasionally.

Marinara Sauce

(serves 6)

¼ cup olive oil
½ cup onion, minced
1 clove garlic, minced
3 cups canned Italian tomatoes, chopped
2 anchovy filets, mashed
½ cup dry white wine
½ tsp. oregano
½ tsp. basil
1 tbsp. parsley, chopped
salt and pepper to taste

Heat oil in a saucepan, sauté onion and garlic until light golden, add all other ingredients and simmer for 30 minutes.

Serve with spaghetti or seafood.

Mushroom Sauce

(for spaghetti or baked noodles)

¼ cup olive oil
1 cup onion, minced
1 clove garlic, minced
¾ lb. mushrooms, sliced thin
¼ lb. cooked ham, minced
2 cups tomato puree
½ cup dry red wine
1 cup beef broth
1 small pinch thyme
salt and pepper to taste

Heat oil in a saucepan, add onion and garlic and sauté until onion is soft; add mushrooms and sauté 5 minutes. Stir in ham and sauté a couple of minutes longer. Add tomato puree, wine, broth, thyme, salt and pepper, mix well and cook gently for about one hour.

Sausage Sauce for Spaghetti

1 lb. Italian sausage, sweet and hot, mixed to taste
¼ cup dry white wine
½ cup onion, minced
1 clove garlic, minced
¼ cup celery, chopped
1 tbsp. parsley, minced
2 cups canned tomatoes
1 cup tomato paste (2 cans)
½ cup beef broth
1 bay leaf
salt and pepper to taste

Prick skin of sausages with a needle, put together with the wine in a saucepan and simmer until the wine has evaporated and the sausages start to sizzle. Add onion, garlic, celery and parsley; sauté, stirring at times, until sausages are browned and onion golden. Add all other ingredients, blend, cover and simmer for an hour.

Italian Tomato Sauce

(6 cups)

(for spaghetti, stews, etc.)

3 tbsp. olive oil
1 cup minced onion
2 cloves garlic, minced
2½ cups canned Italian tomatoes
½ cup tomato paste (small can)
1½ cups chicken broth (or water)
1 tsp. dried basil
¼ tsp. thyme
½ tsp. rosemary
1 bay leaf
1 tsp. sugar
1 tsp. vinegar
salt and pepper to taste
½ cup dry white wine (opt.)

Heat oil in a saucepan, add onion and garlic and sauté until onion is soft. Add all other ingredients, stir well and simmer for 45 minutes. Strain and reheat before serving.

Pesto

(for 6 servings)

2 cups of fresh small basil leaves
½ cup olive oil
3 tbsp. pine nuts
2 large cloves garlic, crushed
1 tsp. lemon juice
salt and pepper to taste
⅓ cup grated parmesan cheese
¼ cup grated romano cheese
2 tbsp. butter

Put basil, oil, pine nuts, garlic, lemon juice, salt and pepper in a blender or food processor and process at high speed until well blended to a smooth paste. Then add grated cheeses, blend at lower speed and finally add the butter and blend again. Just before serving over spaghetti, beat in 2 or 3 tablespoons of hot water.

Spaghetti *al pesto* is one of the greatest pasta dishes. The pesto, a basil sauce, is traditionally prepared by pounding the ingredients in a mortar. A blender or food processor can simplify the preparation considerably.

Apple Fritters

(for 4)

3 or 4 firm apples
1/3 cup sugar
2 tbsp. rum
1 tbsp. maraschino liqueur
1 tbsp. grated lemon rind
pinch of ground cinnamon
1½ tbsp. lemon juice
1 tbsp. grated orange rind
1 cup water
¾ cup flour
pinch of salt
vegetable oil for frying

Peel and core the apples and slice them crosswise into ½ inch thick slices. Blend sugar, rum, maraschino liqueur, lemon rind, orange rind, cinnamon and lemon juice, add apples and mix gently. Let stand for a couple of hours.

Make a batter with flour, water and salt. Put oil to a depth of ½ inch in a heavy skillet. Heat over high flame. Pat apple slices dry, dip them in batter, and fry — a few at a time — in hot oil until brown on one side, turn and brown the other side. Remove from skillet, drain on paper towel and sprinkle with powdered sugar before serving. They should be served piping hot.

Custard with Asti Spumante Sauce

(for 6)

Custard:
6 eggs
$^1/_3$ cup sugar
1 tsp. vanilla
dash of salt
1½ cups light cream
1¾ cups milk

Sparkling Sauce:
1 pint fresh strawberries
3 tbsp. currant jelly
1 tsp. cornstarch
1 tbsp. water
2 tsp. sugar
$^1/_3$ to ½ cup Asti Spumante wine

Custard: Beat together eggs, sugar, vanilla and salt. Stir in cream and milk. Pour into buttered 5½ cup ring mold. Place mold in pan of hot water. Bake in 350° oven for 40 minutes or until knife inserted in center comes out clean. Cool custard. Run spatula around edge of mold to loosen; unmold onto serving plate. Chill until serving time.

Sparkling Sauce: Puree 1 cup of strawberries in electric blender; strain to remove seeds. In small saucepan, melt jelly over low heat. Mix together cornstarch and water to make a smooth paste. Stir into melted jelly with sugar and half the puree; cook and stir until mixture boils 1 minute. Stir in remaining puree and chill. At serving time pour the Asti Spumante into sauce. Garnish custard with remaining strawberries and serve with sauce.

Biscuit Tortoni

(for 8 to 10)

¾ cup sugar
¾ cup water
2 eggs, separated
1 doz. macaroons *(p. 154)* or other almond macaroons, crushed fine
2 tsp. almond extract
1 tbsp. rum
1 ½ cups heavy cream, whipped

Combine water and sugar and cook in a saucepan; boil until the syrup spins a thread — 230° on the thermometer. Remove from fire and cool. Beat egg whites until stiff, gradually mix in the syrup; beat egg yolks until creamy and blend in the syrup mixture along with the almond extract and rum. Reserve two tablespoons of crushed macaroons and mix the others with the syrup, then fold into the whipped cream. Put bowl with the mixture in the freezer for about 30 minutes. When just about frozen, remove, stir well and fill into small paper cups. Sprinkle top with remaining macaroons and freeze overnight.

Fresh Fruit Bowl

(for 6-8)

1 cup dry white wine
3/4 cup fresh orange juice
1/3 cup maraschino liqueur
1 tbsp. grated lemon rind
2 pears
2 apples
1 cup fresh pineapple
about 5 cups other fresh fruits in season such as: melon; peaches, apricots, figs, cherries, seedless grapes, strawberries
6 tbsp. sugar, or to taste

Peel, pare and dice all fruit, except berries or grapes, put in a bowl, mix with all other ingredients, cover and chill 12 hours before serving. Garnish with a few mint leaves or thin slices or orange.

Italian Lemon Ice

(for 8)

1 cup fresh lemon juice
1 cup water
2 cups sugar
1 cup ice water
1 tbsp. grated lemon rind

Combine 1 cup water and the sugar, bring to a boil in a saucepan and cook for 5 minutes, stirring until sugar is well dissolved. Remove from heat and cool. Add all other ingredients, mix and chill. Pour into two or three ice cube trays, place in freezing compartment. Freeze for about 20 minutes or until nearly solidly frozen. Remove, put in a bowl and beat with an electric hand mixer until uniformly mushy. Return to freezer. After about 45 minutes, repeat above procedure. Then freeze for an hour or until quite firm and serve.

Mocha Mousse

(for 6)

6 oz. semi-sweet chocolate
1 tbsp. sugar
4 eggs
¼ cup strong espresso coffee
2 tbsp. strega cordial
2 tbsp. rum
1 cup heavy cream, whipped

Separate eggs. Beat whites until stiff, beat egg yolks with sugar until light and creamy. Melt chocolate in top of a double boiler over simmering water. When melted, remove from heat, blend in egg yolks, coffee, strega and rum, blend well. Fold in egg whites and whipped cream. Put into a serving bowl or individual small cups or demi-tasse cups. Chill well, preferably overnight.

Milan Macaroons

(about 2 dozen)

½ lb. blanched almonds
1½ cups confectioners sugar
½ tsp. vanilla
flour
1 tsp. almond extract
1 tbsp. brandy
2 large egg whites, beaten stiff

Chop almonds, mix with sugar and grind, using the finest blade of a grinder. Blend in vanilla, almond extract and brandy. Fold in beaten egg whites, cover mixture and chill for several hours.

Put wax paper on a cookie sheet, dust lightly with flour and place small spoonfuls of almond mixture on the wax paper. Let rest for an hour, then bake in 325° oven for 20 minutes or until golden brown. Cool on the sheet for 15 minutes before removing. Store in tightly covered jar for a couple of days before serving.

Zuppa Inglese

(for 8)

10-inch sponge cake
6 egg yolks, lightly beaten
1/3 cup sugar
3 tbsp. cornstarch
2 cups milk
pinch of salt
1 tsp. grated lemon rind

½ cup dark rum
¼ cup marsala wine
¼ cup crème de cacao liqueur

For the topping:

1 cup heavy cream, whipped
3 tbsp. candied fruit, chopped

Combine sugar, cornstarch, salt and lemon rind, stir into milk, put in a pan and heat. Put egg yolks in top of a double boiler over simmering water, gradually add milk mixture while beating until the custard has thickened. Remove and chill.

Cut the sponge cake in three layers and place one in a shallow dish or bowl. Sprinkle with crème de cacao and spread one third of custard on top. Cover with second layer of cake. Combine rum and marsala and sprinkle second layer with half the mixture and spread second third of custard on top. Cover with third layer of cake, sprinkle with rum mixture and spread last of custard. Cover with whipped cream and sprinkle candied fruit on top. Chill well before serving.

Ricotta Flambé

(for 6)

1½ lbs. ricotta
¼ cup milk
3 tbsp. sugar
(or to taste)
3 tbsp. brandy
2 tbsp. grated
semi-sweet chocolate
3 tbsp. brandy

Blend ricotta with milk, sugar and 3 tablespoons brandy and beat until smooth and creamy. Put into a serving bowl. Chill for a couple of hours. Just before serving heat remaining brandy, pour over top of cheese and ignite. Spoon cheese into serving cups and sprinkle with grated chocolate.

Coffee Granita

(for 6)

2 cups espresso coffee
3 tbsp. sugar
1 cup heavy cream,
whipped

Dissolve sugar in hot coffee, cool and proceed as in lemon ice. Serve with ample whipped cream.

Peaches with Zabaglione Sauce

(for 4)

4 firm ripe peaches, skinned and halved
½ cup dry white wine
3 tbsp. sugar
2 tbsp. maraschino liqueur
4 slices sponge cake
2 tbsp. candied orange peel, diced
2 cups Zabaglione sauce

Blend wine, sugar, maraschino liqueur. Put halved peaches in bowl, pour wine mixture over them and let stand for an hour. Place a slice of sponge cake on each serving dish, put 2 peach halves on top, cover with Zabaglione sauce and sprinkle with candied orange rind.

Zabaglione Sauce

(about 3 cups)

3 egg yolks
1⅓ cups sugar
⅛ tsp. grated nutmeg
1¾ cups dry marsala wine
¾ cup heavy cream, whipped

Beat egg yolks until creamy, put in top of double boiler with sugar, nutmeg, and marsala; place over simmering water and beat with a hand beater or a whisk until the mixture thickens and is creamy. Remove from fire, and continue beating until the mixture is cool. Fold in whipped cream and serve.

Zabaglione

(for 4)

6 egg yolks
¼ cup sugar
½ cup dry marsala wine

Put egg yolks and sugar in the top of a double boiler and beat with a wire whisk or an electric hand mixer until light yellow and creamy. In the bottom of the double boiler bring water to a simmer, place top over it but do not let touch the water. Continue whisking the egg yolks and gradually beat in the marsala. Beat until the mixture is quite thick, begins to foam and holds its shape.

Remove from heat, spoon into goblets or tulip shaped glasses and serve immediately.

Index

Basic metric conversions

Solid measures

15 grams	=	½ ounce
25 grams	=	1 ounce
50 grams	=	2 ounces
125 grams	=	4 ounces
225 grams	=	8 ounces
450 grams	=	1 pound
1 kilogram	=	2 pounds 2 ounces

Liquid measures

25 millilitres	=	1 fluid ounce
50 millilitres	=	2 fluid ounces
125 millilitres	=	4 fluid ounces
150 millilitres	=	5 fluid ounces
300 millilitres	=	10 fluid ounces
600 millilitres	=	1 pint
1 litre	=	1¾ pints

Linear measures

0·6 centimetre	=	¼ inch
1·3 centimetres	=	½ inch
2·5 centimetres	=	1 inch
10 centimetres	=	4 inches
15 centimetres	=	6 inches
23 centimetres	=	9 inches
30 centimetres	=	1 foot
1 metre	=	40 inches